D0592053

Scenic
Driving
MICHIGAN

Written by Kathy-jo Wargin
Photographs by Ed Wargin

FALCON®

HELENA, MONTANA

A FALCON GUIDE

Falcon® is continually expanding its list of guidebooks. You can order extra copies of this book and get information and prices for other Falcon® books by writing Falcon, P.O. Box 1718, Helena, MT 59624, or by calling 1-800-582-2665. Also, please ask for a free copy of our current catalog listing all Falcon books. To contact us via e-mail, visit our website at http:\\www.falconguide.com.

2 3 4 5 6 7 8 9 0 MG 03 02 01 99

© 1997 by Falcon® Publishing, Inc., Helena, Montana.
Printed in the United States of America.

All rights reserved, including the right to reproduce this book or parts thereof in any form, except for inclusion of brief quotations in a review.

Cover, color insert, and all black-and-white photos by Ed Wargin.

Library of Congress Cataloging-in-Publication Data
Wargin, Kathy-jo.
      Scenic driving Michigan / Kathy-jo and Ed Wargin.
          p.   cm.
      ISBN 1-56044-518-1
      1. Michigan—Guidebooks.   2. Automobile travel—Michigan—
Guidebooks.   I. Wargin, Ed.   II. Title.
      F564.3.W37   1997
      917.7404'43—dc21   97-9802
                                                     CIP

 Text pages printed on recycled paper.

CAUTION

All participants in the recreational activities suggested by this book must assume the responsibility for their own actions and safety. The information contained in this guidebook cannot replace sound judgment and good decision-making skills, which help reduce risk exposure; nor does the scope of this book allow for disclosure of all the potential hazards and risks involved in such activities.

Learn as much as possible about the recreational activities in which you participate, prepare for the unexpected, and be cautious. The reward will be a safer and more enjoyable experience.

Contents

Acknowledgments

We would like to extend sincere thanks to the many people who helped make this adventure possible. First and foremost, the terrific people we met along the way who were more than happy to share their thoughts, ideas, and Michigan secrets with us. We would like to thank the individual chambers of commerce and the Upper Peninsula Travel and Recreation Association for all of their great information.

We would also like to gratefully acknowledge Mike Lussier, owner of Lightstorm Imaging of Michigan, for his never-ending patience and absolute expertise in film processing. Thank you also to friend Richard Hamilton Smith, for his encouragement, support, and, as always, the long glass.

Last, but not least, we would like to thank our wonderful neighbors, Bill and Todd Altier, for watching our dog Otto and minding the fort while we were gone—you are the best neighbors anyone could ask for! And our thanks to Jake Peter Wargin, for being so patient and cooperative throughout the entire project.

About this book

This book is intended as a guide for recreational traveling through the state of Michigan. As you will read, Michigan is a large state brimming with beauty and natural wonders; and it would be nearly impossible to include every scenic drive that exists in such a bountiful region. Many of the drives trace the shores of the Great Lakes, or travel through recreational spots bustling with exciting things to see and do. We hope you will use this book as a way to begin your travels in Michigan, but feel free to venture off the main designations in search of your own nugget of Michigan scenic pleasure.

This book is dedicated to our parents.

Locator Map—*Upper Peninsula*

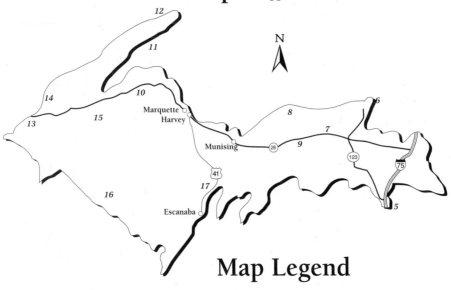

N

12
11
14
10
Marquette
Harvey
15
13
16
17
Munising
Escanaba
8
6
7
9
28
123
75
41
5

Map Legend

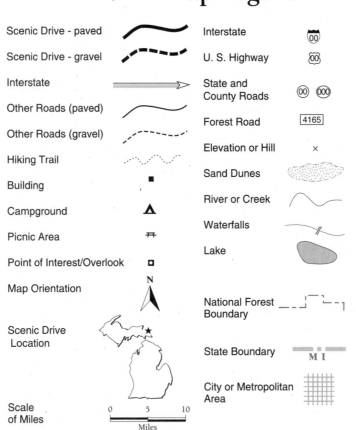

Scenic Drive - paved	Interstate
Scenic Drive - gravel	U. S. Highway
Interstate	State and County Roads
Other Roads (paved)	Forest Road
Other Roads (gravel)	Elevation or Hill
Hiking Trail	Sand Dunes
Building	River or Creek
Campground	Waterfalls
Picnic Area	Lake
Point of Interest/Overlook	
Map Orientation	
Scenic Drive Location	National Forest Boundary
	State Boundary
	City or Metropolitan Area
Scale of Miles	

0   5   10
Miles

Locator Map—*Lower Peninsula*

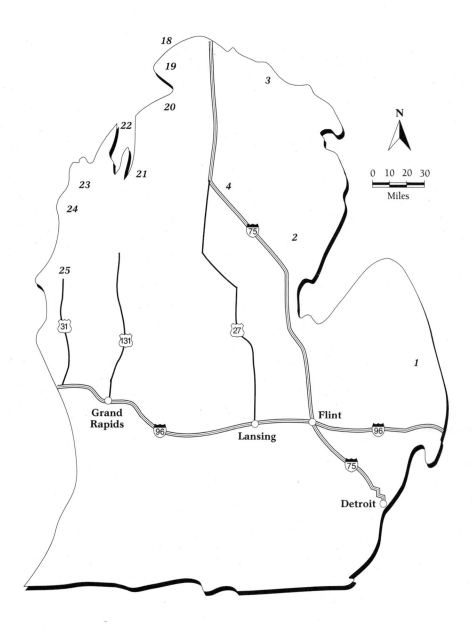

The shoreline of Au Sable Dunes near Grand Marais.
Steep sandy banks spin sand and rock into Lake Superior.

Introduction

The majestic white pine reigns as state tree. The delicate apple blossom, frilly, fragrant, and sweet, holds the title of state flower. The scenic drives in this state of rainbow trout and petoskey stones wind along sandy windswept shores, into thick forests of virgin white pine, and through vast wetlands teeming with lush aquatic plants and wildlife.

Michigan is embraced by four of the Great Lakes, offering more than 3,000 shoreline miles. Lake Michigan lies to the west of Michigan, Lake Superior to the north, Lake Huron to the east, and Lake Erie to the southeast. The state hosts more than 3.9 million acres of state forest land and 2.5 million acres of national forest land, creating one of the best places in the country for viewing wildlife, pristine forest, and unspoiled lakeshore.

The state is formed by two land masses. The northern portion is called the upper peninsula, while the larger, southern portion is referred to as the lower peninsula. The Mackinac Bridge, a 5-mile suspension bridge, connects the two areas, spanning the waterway known as the Straits of Mackinac. The drive from St. Ignace to Cheboygan takes you over this bridge, where you can view the great expanses of Lake Michigan to the west and Lake Huron to the east.

Only ten thousand years ago, the area that is now Michigan was sleeping beneath a blanket of ice. As it retreated, this glacial formation carved huge basins in the earth, leaving puddles of water behind. These depressions, and hilly formations, escarpments, and jagged shores also created by glaciation complete much of the geologic picture that is Michigan today.

From around 1600 to the 1800s, the Ojibwe occupied most of the upper peninsula and eastern portion of the lower peninsula, while the Ottawa occupied the western portion of the lower peninsula. When European settlement began in the region in the early 1600s, the Native Americans were joined by a group of French explorers, missionaries, and trappers. There are over 36,000 miles of rivers and streams in Michigan, waterways once used as highways by French fur traders, who built trading posts along their paths. In the upper peninsula alone, there are more than 100 waterfalls and 4,300 inland lakes. Michigan was a hub for the fur traders, who thrived on trapping beaver.

Sault Ste. Marie, in the upper peninsula, was the cornerstone of Michigan's early development. French explorers portaged there in 1634 when passing through on their explorations for a northwest passage. Several years later Father Jacques Marquette, a Jesuit missionary, founded the first permanent settlement there. In 1671 he moved south and created another settlement, Michigan's second permanent one, near the Straits of Mackinac. It was called Mission Saint Ignace and is now known as St. Ignace.

As the beaver population went into serious decline, logging took over as Michigan's economic flagship. The two areas of land that comprise Michigan were once covered with forest. These trees fed the insatiable hunger of the budding lumber industry during an era known as the "Big Cut." The resulting furniture and carriage-building industry attracted immigrants from Germany, Sweden, Norway, Finland, and Italy in the mid 1800s.

In 1834, Michigan applied for statehood but was denied, due to the fact that a dispute between Michigan and Ohio over a piece of land around Lake Erie, which included the Port of Toledo, was still unsettled. When the Toledo War, as it was called, was resolved, Ohio was given the strip near Lake Erie, and Michigan was given the upper peninsula as compensation.

The upper peninsula was thought of as a remote wasteland of sorts, and it wasn't until copper and iron ore were discovered there that the acquisition of this portion of land showed incomparable economic promise. In 1855 the Soo Locks in Sault Ste. Marie opened, and with the onset of easier travel into the great lakes, the mining industry went full tilt and heavier settling of the area began. By the 1900s, however, the area was depleted of its trees and the economy went bust. Fortunately, at that point the automotive industry arrived to fuel the economy.

Scenic Driving Michigan describes 25 drives through small, charming resort towns with bustling marinas and stately lighthouses, and through thick boreal forests and undulating hills with carpets of bracken fern and trillium. Between Harbor Springs and Cross Village in the northwestern portion of the lower peninsula exists breathtaking natural beauty. As this winding narrow drive elevates you above the shore of Lake Michigan, the deciduous trees form a natural canopy. In autumn, brilliant hues melt into a kaleidoscope of color, with the gentle blueness of Lake Michigan to the east peeking through the leaves.

The mitten-shaped lower peninsula offers diversity among its landscape and its people, offering long sandy beaches that melt into blue-green waters, and fields that produce important agricultural products. The area near Traverse City occupies soil which is perfect for cherry and apple orchards. The drive down the east arm of Traverse Bay runs among lazy sloping orchards of cherry trees. If you arrive at harvest time, you'll pass roadside stands with brown bags of plump, sweet, juicy red cherries. In the center of the upper peninsula sits Seney National Wildlife Refuge. This area was ravaged and left barren by the logging industry that depleted the northwoods of its trees in the late 1800s. Left burned, empty, and scarred, this area was considered nothing more than a vast wasteland and was abandoned by farmers. In the late 1930s, the Civilian Conservation Corps (CCC) created a system of dikes that pooled a marshland area that is now home to more than two hundred species of birds as well as bear, beaver, otter, and deer. The drive through Seney National Wildlife Refuge is a loop drive that takes place on top of the dike system giving close-up views of marshland dedicated to the preservation of wildlife.

Michigan is also a state steeped in the travel industry. In 1818, *Walk-in-the-Water*, a New York-based steamship, docked at Detroit and began the era of steamship travel on the Great Lakes. As a result, the northern portion of the lower peninsula became a vacation hotspot for the wealthy from Chicago and New York. Several of the drives along the northwestern coast of the lower peninsula whisk you through towns where you can enjoy many recreational opportunities, fine shopping, and great dining, too. Petoskey, Charlevoix, Traverse City, and Harbor Springs are wonderful places that reflect the history of Michigan as a summer travel destination.

Michigan may surprise you with the rugged beauty of the upper peninsula and the smooth recreational gloss of the lower peninsula. This state thrives in every season. In summer months, trail hikers, campers, and boaters abound, while snowmobilers, showshoers, and skiers fill the area in the winter.

Drive 1: Port Huron To Tawas City

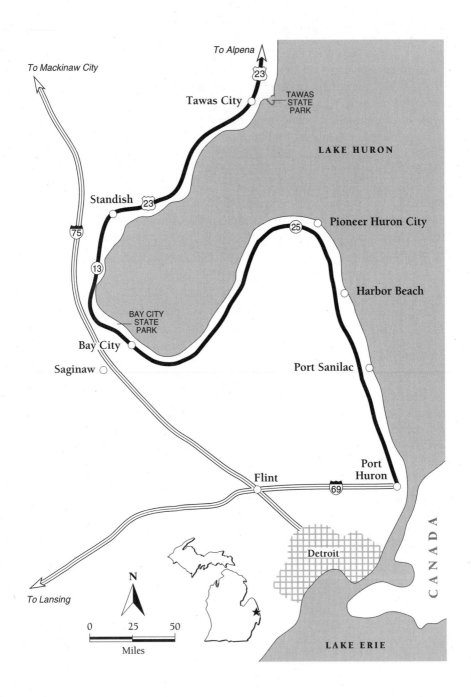

1

Port Huron To Tawas City

General description: This is a drive from Port Huron to Tawas City, through small harbor towns, pretty roadside parks, and quaint villages with Victorian homes and antique shops. This 143-mile drive is unremarkable in terms of natural wonders, but it does offer the adventure of going from town-to-town along what was once an Indian foot path.

Special attractions: Blue Water Bridge, Tawas Point Lighthouse, and Tawas Point Beach.

Location: The east coast of the lower peninsula.

Drive route numbers: Michigan Highway 25, Michigan Highway 13, Michigan Highway 53, Michigan Highway 247, and U.S. Highway 23.

Travel season: Year-round.

Camping: All the way.

Services: Full services entire drive.

 The drive

Part of the Lake Huron Circle Tour, this drive follows the eastern coast of Michigan, next to Lake Huron. The drive begins in the town of Port Huron, which is located in St. Clair County. The St. Clair River, which links the upper and lower Great Lakes, runs through Port Huron. This waterway played an important part in the development of the area. A popular connecting route for fur traders and Indians, the St. Clair River saw a lot of birch bark canoes and explorers in the 1700s.

The city of Port Huron is also the location of an underwater railroad, the world's first, which connects Port Huron to Sarnia, Ontario. This 2,290-foot-long underwater tunnel was completed and operating by 1891. Located south of John Street in Port Huron, the tunnel is still in active service. Railroad cars too large for the tunnel are escorted across the waterway on a large ferry.

Today, Port Huron has a population of about 34,000 people. This area was one of the first settled by the French in the 1600s. In 1686, the French constructed an early outpost, Fort St. Joseph, near here. Fort St. Joseph, the second white settlement in the area, existed to guard the waterway which connects Lake Erie and Lake Huron, and to keep the English out of the upper Great Lakes. In 1687, this fort was the mobilization center for French and Indians who had banded together to wage war on the English. Fort St.

Sanilac County Historical Museum.

Joseph was abandoned by the French in 1688. In 1814, Americans built another fort, Fort Gratiot, on the former site of Fort Joseph, again to keep the British out of Lakes Superior and Huron.

Begin this drive on MI 25 proceeding north out of Port Huron. You will pass the Blue Water Bridge, which spans the St. Clair River at a height of 152 feet—tall enough to allow freighters to pass beneath it. Built in 1938, this bridge connects Port Huron to Sarnia, Ontario.

After 2.5 miles, on the right, you'll find a portion of Lake Port State Park. The trees are so thick here that you cannot see any of Lake Huron, which is just beyond the trees to the right.

As you continue northward on MI 25, you will notice signs designating this drive as a portion of the Lake Huron Circle Tour. This is a self-guided auto tour that follows the most scenic routes along the shores of Lake Huron. For many miles, however, you will not be able to see Lake Huron (still on your right) due to the collections of homes that block the view.

The terrain is fickle here—long, rolling pastures and orchards one moment; closed, thick forests of hardwoods the next. For the next several miles you travel in and out of small villages edged by apple orchards. Eventually, you arrive at Lexington County Park in Sanilac County. A very basic park, it offers simple rental cottages and a nice picnic area. Tall hardwood trees begin to line this portion of the drive.

2

Shortly after passing Lexington County Park, you begin to get vague glimpses of Lake Huron to your right as the area between the road and the shore opens up a bit. A few miles farther you are exposed to a wonderful view of Lake Huron.

Three more miles and you're in the village of Port Sanilac. Watch for a reduced speed limit in this area. Sanilac is home to both the Sanilac County Historical Museum and the Port Sanilac Light, built in 1886. Originally a white light fueled by kerosene, the color of the light was changed to red in 1889. Eventually, it was replaced by a flashing electric light.

After passing through Sanilac, you break into wide open pastures on your left, while to your right homes dot the shoreline and obstruct the view of the lake. After 5 miles you come to Forester, and Forester County Park, which has a simple beach.

Past the park, the area is again graced with large open pastures, showing the agricultural mix of the area. Cornfields and contented cows can be spotted from this section of the drive. Not far beyond Forester County Park there is a scenic turnout with picnic table and restrooms. This is an overlook of Lake Huron and the small, simple beaches below. The road continues through an area filled with pine and cedar trees, interspersed with cornfields and pastures. It is at this point that you begin to break into consistently better views of Lake Huron.

After 15 miles you approach the area of Harbor Beach, birthplace of Frank Murphy. Murphy was a Michigan governor who would not use the National Guard to put an end to a 1937 sit-down strike at the General Motors plant in Flint. His decision paved the way for the creation of the United Auto Workers Union of America. Here, you can visit the Murphy home, which remains much as it was in the 1920s when Murphy lived there.

Just out of Harbor Beach the road begins to straighten and is lined with hardwood trees such as maple and elm. After 6.4 miles you will arrive at Port Hope, a lovely Victorian town known for its antique shops and quaint churches. Just out of Port Hope the area spreads into an open rural scene on the right as MI 25 begins to veer away from the Lake Huron shore.

Proceeding north, you pass Bald Eagle Point on your right and within a few minutes come to Huron City at the eastern tip of Michigan's "thumb." The lower peninsula of Michigan is shaped like a mitten; Huron City, in Huron County, and Sanilac County are located in the thumb area of the mitten. These two counties suffered from a severe forest fire in 1881. The 3-day inferno burned more than 1 million acres and killed at least 125 people.

Passing through Huron City, MI 25 continues to veer from the shore and takes you about 2.3 miles northwest, then about 6 miles due west to Port Austin, where MI 25 intersects with MI 53. At the intersection, turn right and take MI 53 into the heart of Port Austin, situated at the western tip of the "thumb." After a 1 mile drive into the middle of town, turn left on MI

An old building in historic Huron City.

25 and proceed along the shore. Shortly thereafter, you will pass Port Crescent State Park, situated 4 miles southwest of Port Austin.

Several miles later, traveling south now, you pass through the Rush Lake State Game Area on your left, while you can view Lake Huron to your right. Only 2 miles later you come to Albert Sleeper State Park, located on your left. Sleeper State Park is filled with dense trees and offers swimming and a boat launch.

Continue along MI 25 now for a spell as you make your way around to the base of Saginaw Bay. The road will again veer away from the shore for several miles and will eventually take you into the large town of Bay City, located about 3 miles south of the bay. Bay City was once an Ojibwe Indian camp. More than one hundred years ago, a man named Leon Tromble, who was in the area on assignment for the federal government, built a small log home on the banks of the Saginaw River. His homesteading made way for Bay City, which eventually became a successful lumber town.

The Sage Mill, Bay City's first lumber mill, was erected in 1865. At the height of the lumber boom in the late 1880s, there were more than fifty mills in Bay City. By 1888, more than 4 billion board feet of lumber had been cut in Bay City. Ten years later, a salt basin lying beneath Bay City's soil was tapped, and a new industry was born.

As you make your way into Bay City you will cross the Saginaw River. The East Michigan Tourist Association is located at the riverside. This is a recommended stop for anyone vacationing along Michigan's east side. You will find brochures and information about the area's highlights and its roads. City Hall is to the left of MI 25 (at 301 Washington Avenue) at the bank of the river. It houses the Chmielewska Tapestry. This tapestry, which measures 9 by 30 feet, was woven by a Polish born artist and portrays city landmarks. The city hall is, itself, a beautiful sight. It is a romanesque style building built in the late 1800s, boasting a 125-foot-tall clock tower, intricate woodwork, and metal pillars. It is listed on the National Register of Historic Places. Next to the city hall is the Kantzler Memorial Arboretum, which holds native trees and bushes as well as wonderful historic displays.

As you cross the river, you will pass Veteran's Memorial Park to your right. Shortly after, you will come to MI 13. Turn right on MI 13 and proceed north to Bay City State Park, which is located on the shore of the bay. In a few miles, there is a fork in the road. MI 13 continues on the left fork; the right fork is MI 247. You should bear right on MI 247. This leads directly to the state park. There are several good swimming beaches at this state park. At the park the road veers left to head north along the upper edge of the bay. To return to the main drive route, on MI 13, head west on Beaver Road out of the park. Turn north on MI 13. The next 20 miles or so are unremarkable, except for some random views of the lake.

Once you are back on MI 13, continue heading north toward the town of Au Gres. Shortly after entering Arenac County, US 23 joins MI 13 from the left. (From this point on, the road is referred to as US 23.) Arenac County was named by a man named Henry Schoolcraft in 1840. The word *arenac* is derived from Latin and means "a sandy place." Before reaching Au Gres, you reach the village of Omer, which is 8 miles inland. Here, the road takes a sharp turn to the right and heads directly toward the shore and the town of Au Gres. From there, the road curves gently to the north, mirroring the shoreline all the way to Tawas.

From Au Gres to Tawas Point, an area of about 20 miles, you pass more than ten beaches and parks, all on the shore of Lake Huron's Saginaw Bay, which is on your right. As you enter Tawas City, the end of this drive, you will round the curve of Tawas Bay to find Tawas Point State Park. The state park is located off US 23, 2.5 miles south of East Tawas on Tawas Beach Road. This park offers a modern campground and picnic area on the shore of Lake Huron. The Tawas Point Lighthouse is located in the park. It is open to the public by appointment only because Coast Guard personnel live there. This tower was built in 1876 and towers 70 feet above the shore of Lake Huron.

Drive 2: Lumberman's Monument Auto Tour

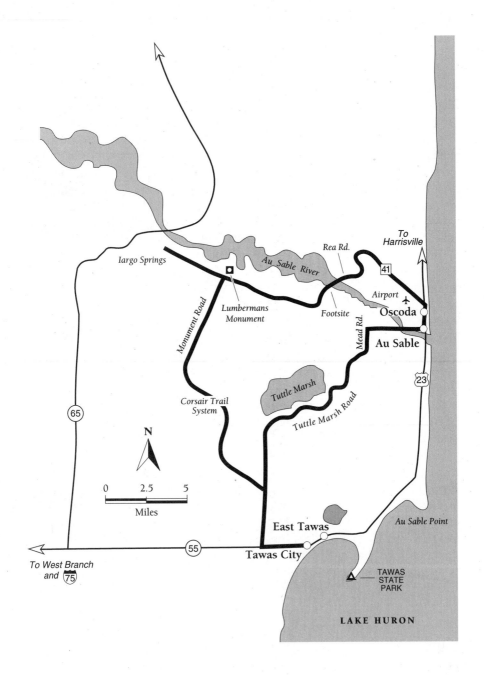

2

Lumberman's Monument Auto Tour

General description: This drive begins and ends just west of Tawas City, which is located on the eastern coast of the lower peninsula. The drive, a 68-mile loop, takes you through broadleaf forests, a red pine plantation, and stops at several monuments including the stunning Lumberman's Monument, a tall bronze sculpture depicting the "river rats" who drove logs down the mighty Au Sable River. You also visit serene Iargo Springs, a fresh spring that percolates water from the forest floor right into the Au Sable River. You end the loop drive by proceeding through Tuttle Marsh, a wetland dedicated to the preservation of waterfowl and wildlife habitats.

Special attractions: Corsair Recreation Area, Lumberman's Monument, Canoe Racer's Monument, Iargo Springs, Au Sable River, Foote Dam Overlook, and Tuttle Marsh.

Location: The mid-eastern region of the lower peninsula.

Drive route numbers: Michigan Highway 55, U.S. Highway 23, Monument Road, Wilber Road, River Road, Bissonette Road, Au Sable Road, and County Road F41.

Travel season: Year-round. Note that the Lumberman's Monument Visitor Center is opened only from Memorial Day weekend through Labor Day, from 10 A.M. to 7 P.M. daily.

Camping: Lumber Monument Campground, Van Etten Lake Campground.

Services: Available, for the most part, only at the beginning of drive at the intersection of US 23 and MI 55.

Nearby attractions: Oscoda Beach, Sturgeon Point, Huron National Forest, Tawas Point State Park.

 ## The drive

This drive begins just west of Tawas City, which is located on the eastern coast of the lower peninsula. Access to this drive is possible in several ways. If you are arriving from south of Tawas City, drive north on US 23 to Tawas City and turn left onto MI 55; 1 mile later turn right on Wilber Road. From the north, travel southward on US 23 and turn right on MI 55 to Wilber Road.

The intersection of US 23 and MI 55 is a good place to get gas and refreshments. There are few service places on this drive, and if you visit each monument, it is possible to be on the drive for a couple of hours.

Traveling north on Wilber Road, you will pass through a residential area situated in a forest of cedar and pine. After about 1.5 miles, turn left onto Monument Road, which runs at a slight northwest angle for the next several miles through a mixed hardwood forest.

The road soon emerges into an agricultural area, and gently follows along a hill that quickly elevates you over this agricultural area into a heavy stand of hardwood trees. Four miles later you are still tucked away in the same portion of road. Gradually, the road incorporates more movement with lazy, quarter-mile sways that rock you back and forth through the pine trees.

After 1.5 more miles, you can turn left or right into the Corsair Area, a recreational area neatly tucked into a blanket of pine trees. Open year-round, this area offers toilets, picnic tables, and grills. The Corsair offers more than 26 miles of trails maintained by the Tawas Area Chamber of Commerce and the Corsair Trail Council. During winter months, the Corsair becomes a favorite spot for cross-country skiers and snowshoers. It offers diverse challenges for the expert, and pure comfort for the beginner. During summer months the area is busy with hikers, joggers, and walkers. No bicycles are allowed on the trails. The Corsair, also known for its fine fishing, allows camping, as long as sites are 100 feet from any trail and 200 feet from lakes or streams.

As you leave one of the three Corsair parking areas, turn north onto

The Lumberman's Monument.

Monument Road. You are quickly embraced by thick stands of pine trees. This portion of the drive is spectacular in winter, as icy-draped boughs of pine bend beneath the weight of freshly fallen snow, creating a muted effect.

In 3 miles, you arrive at the Kiwanis Monument, visible to your right. The stones in the monument, carved with names of contributors, came from all portions of Michigan. This monument was erected in 1931 to honor the Kiwanis of Michigan for donating 7 million red pine seedlings planted by the USDA Forest Service. The result of this planting effort, which took place between 1928 and 1930, is the forest of red pine that now dominates nearly 10,000 acres. Red pine, or Norway pine as it is sometimes called, thrives in the well-drained soils of mixed forests. Approximately 70 to 80-feet tall, these trees add one row of branches per year. As you pass this pine plantation, the drive continues through a brief patch of homes and then north to the Lumberman's Monument.

Dedicated in 1932, Lumberman's Monument looms 14 feet in height and is carved completely from bronze. Rising 9 feet above its base, the statue depicts three important figures of the logging era—the sawyer, the river driver, and the timber cruiser. The three appear to be overlooking the formidable Au Sable River.

The impetus for this tribute to all the Michigan lumbermen who dedicated their lives to pushing logs down the mighty Au Sable came from R. G. Schreck of East Tawas. A former supervisor of Huron National Forest, Schreck wanted to create a lasting tribute to the memory of the Michigan logging era. In 1929, he gathered a group of men who were representatives for the largest lumber families of the area, and began taking collections. By 1930, Schreck had collected $44,000 for the memorial, which ultimately cost $50,000. You will notice the names of donors carved into the statue's granite base. The Civilian Conservation Corps built the small log comfort station near the monument and landscaped the grounds.

As you drive out of the parking lot you will see a stop sign at River Road. Travel west on River Road for 1.5 miles to Canoe Race Monument, a monument to honor all marathon canoe racers. This stone monument, crowned with canoe paddles, was originally proposed as a tribute to the late Jerry Curley, who lost his life practicing for the Au Sable River Canoe Marathon. This is a good spot to stop and take in the breathtaking beauty of the area, thick with pristine forest.

Leaving the canoe monument, turn right on River Road and travel west for 1 mile to one of nature's finest mystic places—Iargo Springs. These springs have been called Iargo for more than four hundred years. *Iargo* is the Ojibwe Indian name for "many waters." This was a popular resting spot for the Ojibwe and the French fur traders. There are more than two hundred steps leading down to the springs. These are old wooden steps with places

The Au Sable River was once a major waterway for the lumber industry.

to stop and rest occasionally as you travel down through a dense mature forest, finally arriving at the pine-strewn floor where crystal-clear waters flow from the ground.

Surrounded by thick cedar trees, lichen covered pine trees, and soft green ferns, the view is magical if not mystical. The beautiful Au Sable River flows in the background, adding to the beautiful natural palette. You may also notice hundreds of intricate spiderwebs hanging among the ferns and the fronds. The moisture of the area makes good habitat for creating these sticky webs, and it is easy to spot them.

As you leave Iargo Springs, head east (going back the way you came) on River Road and continue straight through the intersection of River Road and Monument Road. You are now driving alongside the Au Sable River. A scenic overlook offers views of Michigan's longest river. A fine trout stream and recreational river, the Au Sable offers miles of breathtaking beauty and primitive forest. Once a main waterway for Native Americans, French fur traders, trappers, and loggers, the Au Sable of today provides electrical power, and functions as a major recreational outlet.

Leaving the scenic overlook, head east on River Road again for a few miles to Foote Dam. This dam, built in 1917, is one of six dams built by Consumer Power Company on the Au Sable River; the others are the Mio, the Alcona, the Loud, the Five Channels, and the Cooke.

As you leave the dam site, travel northeast on Rea Road. Follow Rea to Bissonette Road. Turn right and proceed along County Road F41. As you travel along CR F41, you will pass the former Paul B. Wurtsmith Air Force Base, home of the Strategic Air Command's 379th Bombardment Wing. The base closed in June of 1993 and is now used by private businesses and industries.

Continue following CR F41 until you merge with US 23. Turn right at the intersection of River Road. As you travel on River Road, to your left will be Eagle Run Ski Area and Nature Trails, 11 miles of chipped trails that follow the Au Sable River's south bank. The hiking trails are well groomed for year-round use, and the area is available for cross-country skiing during winter months.

Follow River Road to Mead Road and turn left. You will notice the area here has been burned, victim of a 1984 forest fire that ravaged over two hundred acres of hardwood and pine trees. Continue following Mead Road to Old US 23 and turn right. Travel for approximately 2 miles, and then turn left onto Tuttle Marsh Road.

This last portion of the drive takes you through a marshland habitat, swollen with swamp grasses and moist aquatic plants. The Tuttle Marsh Wildlife Area is five thousand acres managed by the USDA Forest Service. The creation of this wetland was a goal of the Huron-Manistee National

Iargo Springs percolates delicate quantities of water through deep forest.

Forest. It became a reality from matching funds contributed by Ducks Unlimited's M.A.R.S.H. program, which provided more than $134,000 of the $270,000 it took to create the marsh. Today, improvement projects at the marsh have been completed by The Michigan Wildlife Habitat Foundation, Ducks Unlimited, and the Michigan Department of Natural Resources.

This large wetland contains over 35 miles of a level ditch network and a 2.5-mile low-head dam with water level control structures. With more than thirty-five earthen nesting islands, the area is prime habitat for waterfowl such as several species of duck, Canada geese, and loons. Signs of the health of this wetland include bulrushes, cattails, and lily pads. Characterized by submergent plants near the outer edges, and submergent and free-floating plants toward the deep middle waters of the marsh, this kind of wetland provides food and shelter for many animals. Dawn and dusk are the best times to spot wildlife, and the prime seasons for wildlife and birdwatching are late spring and fall. It is a good idea to check with the Huron Shores Ranger Station in spring and winter; bad weather may render the gravel road impassable.

Leaving the marsh area, turn right onto Swan Road, then left onto May Road. Proceed on to Sherman Road, and turn left. Take a right on Grabow. Follow Grabow and turn left on Wilber Road. Continue south to the intersection of Wilber and MI 55. This places you at the northwest edge of Tawas City, where you began this drive. From here, you can continue on Wilber into Tawas City, or turn left onto MI 55 and head southeast to the Saginaw Bay shore. You can then turn left and travel northeast along the shore about 2 miles to East Tawas. See Drive 3 for more about the Tawas City-East Tawas area.

3

East Tawas to Cheboygan

Lower Peninsula's Northeastern Coast

General description: This drive explores the coastline of the lower peninsula's northeast shore. It begins in East Tawas, proceeds north parallel to Lake Huron past several parks, the Jesse Besser Natural area and the Presque Isle Lights. The beautiful and peaceful Cheboygan State Park lies at the end of the drive.

Special attractions: Harrisville State Park, Sturgeon Point Light, Huron National Forest, Au Sable State Forest, Thunder Bay Underwater Preserve, Alpena, Besser Bell Natural Area, Old Presque Isle and Presque Isle Lighthouse, Thompson's Harbor State Park, Rogers City, Forty Mile Point Light, Cheboygan State Park.

Location: The northeast coast of the lower peninsula.

Drive route numbers: U.S. Highway 23 North, Black River Road, Sandhill Trail, Old State Road.

Travel season: Year-round.

Camping: Harrisville State Park, Thompson's Harbor State Park, P. J. Hoeft State Park, Cheboygan State Park.

Services: Good restaurants, hotels, and shopping line the entire drive.

Nearby attractions: Mackinaw City, Van Riper State Park, Lumberman's Monument Auto Tour.

 The drive

Begin on US 23 in the heart of East Tawas. From the west, you can access US 23 by taking MI 55 into the heart of Tawas City and turning north onto US 23, proceeding into East Tawas.

Begin your drive heading north on US 23 out of East Tawas. Turn right onto Tawas Point Road and follow it for 2 miles to its end. This is Tawas Point, a short piece of land that juts into Lake Huron. Here you will find Tawas Point State Park, Tawas Point Light, and Tawas Point Beach. This area is good for swimming, fishing, and boating, but like most coast cities and beach areas, it can be especially busy during the peak of summer. Now, travel back on Tawas Point Road and turn right to continue north on US 23.

Seven miles north of East Tawas you are traveling on a paved highway through a mixed forest of pine. Soon you begin to see Lake Huron between the trees on the right, and the next few miles offer additional glimpses of Lake Huron, although the view is mostly of homes, cottages, and campgrounds on both sides of the highway. Eventually, beautiful pine trees grace the area, and you will be treated to a vision of "Great Lakes life" as you pass a large array of campsites and marinas.

Four miles later, US 23 takes you through the little town of Au Sable where the mighty Au Sable River empties into Lake Huron after its long journey across much of Michigan. Another 0.5 mile delivers you to the small vacation town of Oscoda, home to the long, quiet shores of Oscoda Beach right on Lake Huron. Continue heading north. Two miles out of Oscoda you will pass Van Etten Lake to your left (west). At that point US 23 will cling closer to Lake Huron's shore.

After about 8 miles you begin to see cottages to your left, and soon the Cedar Lake Access will appear. This is a very busy area, filled with resorts, cars, beachgoers, and tourists. In another 3.5 miles the topography becomes rather undeveloped, and you are escorted away from views of the lake.

Continuing north on US 23, you will approach Harrisville after about 3.5 miles, and break into better views of the shoreline. The entrance to Harrisville State Park is another mile down the road. Next, you venture through the small town of Harrisville, a quaint tourist village with a park and a handful of campgrounds.

The Sturgeon Point Light and Beach on Sturgeon Point will be on your right, about 6 miles north of Harrisville. As you pass this area, proceeding north, the landscape on both sides of the road will begin to be marshy. The Huron National Forest is to your right, and here US 23 begins to curve northwest to proceed farther inland.

Five miles later, the Au Sable State Forest appears to your right. Between the forest and the shore is a small area called the Negwegon State Park which boasts edges stitched with rocky outcroppings that hug small, private coves. There are 10 miles of walking and hiking trails in the interior and near the shoreline, but there is no camping. You can reach the park by turning right off US 23 onto Black River Road, then turning left onto Sandill Trail. This is a sandy road, so drive carefully for the next 2.5 miles. The park entrance will be on your right.

Back out on US 23 proceeding north, you will drive along the coast of Lake Huron's Thunder Bay for about 20 miles until you reach the city of Alpena, a scenic town that overlooks Thunder Bay. This working-class town bears a rich history. In the early 1900s, as the lumber industry went into serious decline, a group of lumbermen began to use the area's rich deposits—pure limestone, marl, shale, and clay—to make portland cement. Their business was a success. Before long, competitor Herman Besser and his son, Jesse, joined the ranks. The Besser Company eventually become the largest cement plant in the world, creating the machines needed to make concrete

Drive 3: East Tawas to Cheboygan
Lower Peninsula's Northeastern Coast

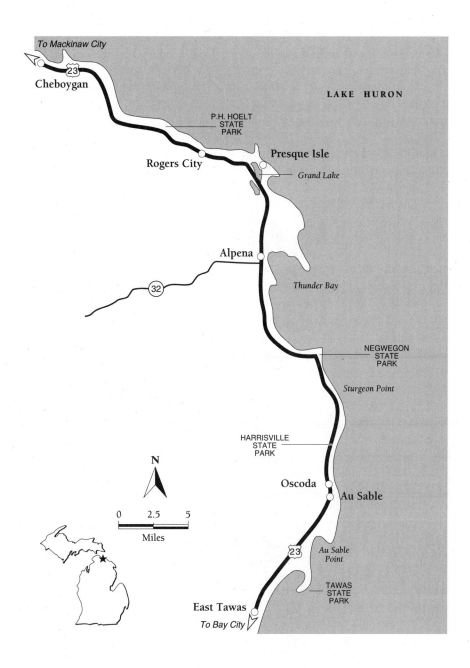

To Mackinaw City

23

Cheboygan

LAKE HURON

P.H. HOELT
STATE
PARK

Presque Isle

Rogers City

Grand Lake

Alpena

32

Thunder Bay

NEGWEGON
STATE
PARK

Sturgeon Point

HARRISVILLE
STATE
PARK

N

Oscoda

Au Sable

0   2.5   5

Miles

23

*Au Sable
Point*

TAWAS
STATE
PARK

East Tawas

To Bay City

blocks, and is still the world's leading producer of this machinery.

The Alpena area was active and economically sound for many years due to the cement factory and employment from paper mills and Wurtsmith Air Force Base. The local economy was able to thrive well into the 1970s without making strides toward a tourism-based economy. But when the air force base closed in 1992, and the cement plant came under new ownership employing fewer than half of what it once had, the area began to experience some hard times. Today, many retired people live in the area.

Good places to visit in Alpena include the Jesse Besser Museum and Planetarium and the Thunder Bay Underwater Preserve. Two miles northwest of Alpena, the Jesse Besser Museum is home to the magnificent Haltiner Collection of Indian artifacts, boasting more than twenty thousand pieces of some of the best Indian artifacts in the country. This collection also contains "copper culture" artifacts more than seven thousand years old that were discovered in the area.

The nearby Thunder Bay Underwater Preserve, which is more than 288 square miles of underwater shipwreckage, contains more than 80 shipwrecks, 15 of which can be investigated by modern day divers. There are twenty dive sites to the schooners, steamers, and barges that lie motionless in Lake Huron's grip, but because this area was designated a preserve in 1981, artifacts are not allowed to be removed from it.

Back on US 23, after traveling north another 8 miles, Long Lake

Tawas Point Lighthouse.

appears to your left, as you near Presque Isle County. To your right are a few rural farms and fields. Presque Isle County—*presque isle* means "almost an island"—was organized in 1871.

After about 6 miles, turn right on Rayburn Highway. Travel nearly 2 miles past the intersection of East Grand Lake Road to the entrance of the Besser Bell Natural Area, to your right. Here, you will find stands of virgin white pine trees, a sandy beach, and walking paths that wind through a dark, eerie cedar forest.

When you leave the Besser Bell Natural Area, turn left onto East Grand Lake Road to proceed north along Grand Lake. This portion of road is wedged neatly between Grand Lake and the shore of Lake Huron. The beaches here are carpeted with broken pieces of fossilized limestone. At this point you will see a piece of land to your right called False Presque Isle. Sitting in the water of Lake Huron, it is separated from the mainland by a channel or bay called the False Presque Isle Harbor. Proceeding north, you will pass the limestone quarry of the Presque Isle Corporation, to your right.

About 4.5 miles farther, as you continue to pass Grand Lake on your left and Lake Esau appears on your right, you will come to a Y in the road. Highland Pines Road veers to the left. Stay to your right to continue north on East Grand Lake Road. You will enter an area filled with charm, nostalgia, and strength. This is the area of Presque Isle Harbor that is home to the Old Presque Isle Lighthouse—the first lighthouse to your right as you round the corner of Presque Isle Harbor.

In the mid 1800s, this was the best port open to sailors on the Great Lakes. The lighthouse was constructed and officially lit in 1840. For thirty years it safely directed ships through this area, until 1870, when a taller lighthouse, called Presque Isle Lighthouse, was built 1 mile down the road at the very end of North Point. The Old Presque Isle Lighthouse was restored in the early 1900s. In 1995 the lighthouse was acquired by the Presque Isle Township with assistance from the Michigan Natural Resources Trust Fund Program and private donors. This area is now a park everyone can enjoy. The lighthouse is filled with antiques and lighthouse artifacts such as a fresnel lens made in France. You can also scurry up the tower for a sweeping view of the lake and the harbor.

The newer Presque Isle Lighthouse and Museum is located in a one hundred acre township park. It is a lovely place to picnic. The soil here contains a high lime content, creating a good habitat for the endangered blue pitcher thistle plant. Pitcher plants grow in wet, soggy soil. In a typical bog, decomposition happens very slowly, which allows only tiny amounts of nitrate to reach the roots of plants. The pitcher plant compensates for this by holding water in its leafstalk where insects converge to find the source of an alluring smell. Forced down the leafstalk by thick hairs, the insect is killed by a narcotic and decomposed from the bacteria. This allows enzymes to convert this protein to nitrogen. There are some insects that seem immune to the ploys of the pitcher plant, such as flesh flies and mosquitoes. You can recognize this plant by its pitcher-shaped leaves, embroidered with red veins. Standing about one to two feet tall, the plant has purple-to-burnt-red colored flowers.

As you leave the Presque Isle area and head back south along North Point, turn right onto Old State Road and follow it west to US 23. About 1 mile before you reach the intersection of US 23 and Old State Road, you will see Thompson's Harbor State Park to your right. This is a great place for cross-country skiing, hiking, and viewing wildflowers. It is a delicate and beautiful natural area, known as the largest concentrated area of Dwarf Lake irises in the world.

Proceed back on Old State Road. When you come to US 23, turn right and head north along US 23. From here, it is about 12 miles to Rogers City, home of the Michigan Limestone and Chemical Company which formally began operations in 1910. Limestone is abundant is this area because in ancient times, warm seas covered Michigan producing many coral-forming organisms, which gradually compressed as they accumulated. These compressions created large limestone deposits such as the Dundee in Rogers City. This compression, which is only 250 feet of stratum, took more than 300 million years to form.

Dense patches of bulrushes are prominent at Cheboygan State Park.

Lakeside Park at Rogers City Harbor has a charming picnic area and sandy beach. There are three beaches west of Rogers City along US 23. All of these beaches are graced with sandy shores and low, velvet dunes. The area here is much softer and kinder to barefeet beachgoers than some of the broken-up and stony shores of southern Michigan.

Head north out of Rogers City to Seagull Point Park, where you can pick up a trailhead for a 2-mile hike. Just across the road from this park is the Herman Vogler Nature Preserve, a pristine, quiet area along the Trout River. No vehicles are allowed in the preserve itself, but there is parking nearby.

Six miles out of Rogers City you arrive at P. J. Hoeft State Park, on your right. This park has more than 140 campsites beneath a canopy of hardwood trees. There is also a mile-long beach which seems deposited into a backdrop of softly mounded dunes, as well as a trail loop of 1.2 miles that takes you along the backside of the dunes.

One mile farther along US 23 is the Forty Mile Point Light to your right, protecting the area near Manitou Beach, which extends northward along the coast. As you drive north for another mile, you will find Evergreen Beach to your right, another place where Lake Huron's waves have created a sandy shore.

A few more miles north of Hoeft is Presque Isle County Lighthouse Park, which boasts a generous picnic area tucked beneath the light green understory of white birch. The Forty Mile Point Lighthouse overlooks the sandy beach here. Although this lighthouse is not open to the public, it adds character and charm to the tranquil setting of these parks and picnic areas.

As you venture a few miles farther on US 23, you begin to round the soft edge of Hammond Bay to your right, while the area to your left becomes increasingly marshlike.

The rest of the road (about 23 miles) to Cheboygan remains quite swampy and moist, mixed with portions of thick forest and Lake Huron shoreline. Two miles south of the actual city of Cheboygan, you will arrive at Cheboygan State Park. Turn right into the park entrance. This park offers camping, hiking trails, and a wide range of wildlife viewing. It is a low wetland area filled with egrets, Canada geese, and many varieties of wetland wildlife.

Just a short drive down US 23 lies the town of Cheboygan, described in Drive 5.

Drive 4: Hartwick Pines State Park

Virgin Pines Scenic Drive

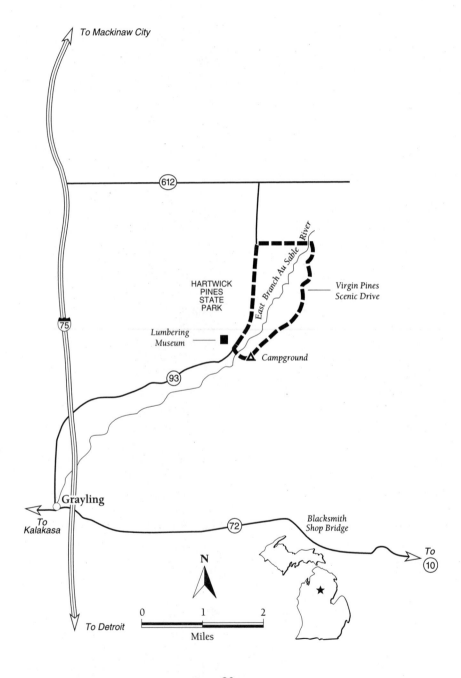

To Mackinaw City

612

To Detroit

75

93

HARTWICK
PINES
STATE
PARK

Lumbering
Museum

East Branch Au Sable River

Virgin Pines
Scenic Drive

Campground

Grayling

To
Kalakasa

72

Blacksmith
Shop Bridge

To
10

N

0   1   2
Miles

4

Hartwick Pines State Park
Virgin Pines Scenic Drive

General description: This 8-mile, one-way loop drive meanders through Hartwick Pines State Park—a stand of virgin pine, a climax forest, a red pine plantation—and crosses the East Branch-Au Sable River twice. An educational experience in the different components of forest life, this drive is quiet and filled with wildlife.

Special attractions: Visitor center, logging museum, Virgin Pines Foot Trail, Au Sable River Foot Trail, and the Mertz Grade Foot Trail.

Location: Crawford County, northeast of Grayling in the north-central portion of the lower peninsula.

Drive route numbers: Interstate 75, Michigan Highway 93.

Travel season: Year-round, but call for information regarding hours for the Michigan Forests Visitor Center and the Logging Camp Museum and campground.

Camping: Modern campgrounds, some sites have full hook-up capabilities. A toilet and shower building is also available. Permits are required, and must be obtained at the ranger office in the park.

Services: None on the Scenic Drive.

Nearby attractions: Petoskey State Park, Traverse City, Mackinaw City.

 The drive

One of the many fine features of Hartwick Pines State Park is the scenic drive through the virgin pines forest. This 8-mile loop winds its way through some of the largest and oldest white pine trees in the state.

Hartwick Pines State Park, the largest state park in the lower peninsula, boasts an area of over 9,672 acres. Rolling hills, small lakes, and unique timber stands comprise this area. The actual "Virgin Pines" forest was donated to the state of Michigan in 1927 by Mrs. Karen B. Hartwick in memory of her husband, Major Edward Hartwick.

Located in the middle upper third of the lower peninsula, you can get to Hartwick Pines State Park by traveling on I-75 and exiting on MI 93. Follow signs to the park. "Big Wheels," a giant logging machine that was used to pull logs out of the woods, will greet you at the park's entrance. Before proceeding to the Virgin Pines Scenic Drive, take some time to stop in at the Michigan Forest Visitor Center. Dedicated to the wildlife that exists in the area, as well as the history of the lumber era and its barons, the visitor center has fine educational exhibits and a balcony that overlooks a portion of white pine forest. The logging museum is filled with artifacts and photographs that tell the story of Michigan's lumbering history. There are foot paths and bicycle paths; check at the visitor's center for maps and background information.

The Virgin Pines Scenic Drive serves as a wonderful educational experience for adults and children by providing the opportunity to see forest growth in different stages. Signs along the trail explain the different stages of growth as well as the variety of wildlife that exists throughout the acreage.

The drive is on a narrow one-car lane, snaking down into a hard-packed dirt road. Coyote, bobcat, black bear, and whitetail deer call the forty-nine-acre stand of timber their home. Drive slowly and carefully, keeping a watchful eye for the forest's most beautiful residents.

After 1.5 miles you cross an old rickety bridge that spans the East Branch-Au Sable River. This branch of the 240-mile river is well known for fine trout fishing and wonderful canoeing opportunities. The Au Sable and all of its tributaries are managed by the state of Michigan, which designates this a natural river, as well as a state-designated wild and scenic river. This river is inhabited by brook trout, and the dense brush along the river banks

Red wagon wheels mark the entrance to Hartwick Pines State Park.

Marker among climax forest maples on Virgin Pines Trail in Hartwick Pines State Park.

provide food and shelter for many of the other area inhabitants such as duck, beaver, mink, and otter.

Continue past the bridge and curve gently along the trail into a considerable stand of virgin jack pine. This tree of the boreal forest is set in dry, sterile, acidic soil. This particular stand has never been cut and may someday be taken over by other types of trees.

The virgin jackpine is noted for its tall straight trunks and small crown. Jack pine, a soft weak wood, was used in making cardboard during the heyday of the lumbering era. The road continues through this stand for about 1 mile.

Driving about 2 more miles, you enter a section of the drive called the "mixed forest." The road is still narrow, and to fully appreciate the intricate beauty of such a mixed forest it is best to continue to drive slowly. This section of forest was all naturally seeded from hemlock (which can reach an age of more than five hundred years), by tamarack, by red maple with its vibrant leaves and dark gray trunk (much loved by deer), and by white and red pine trees. You will also spy white spruce, which is usually found on edges of streams and is characterized by soft needles and cylindrical cones.

At approximately 5 miles into the trail, you cross the East Branch-Au Sable River once more. This section of the river is nothing more than a gently percolating stream. Neither large nor fast, this shallow and exceptionally clear water boasts a beautiful rocky, silty bottom.

The next portion of the loop is the Red Pine Plantation. Red pine thrives best in sandy soils and gravel, and is identified by long needles that appear in clusters of two, and a trunk cloaked in reddish, flaky bark. Red pines grow quickly—up to one foot per year—until they are sixty or seventy years old, then growth declines. Many red pines can reach an age of three hundred or more years.

This particular stand was planted in the mid-1930s by the Civilian Conservation Corps to replenish the area which was severely depleted by logging. Michigan led the country in tree planting with a total of 485 million plantings.

The dense uppermost foliage lets in little, if any, sunlight. This lack of sunlight inhibits new growth. With little or no new growth, the forest floor remains bare, sparse, and offers no food or forage for wildlife.

As you near the end of the trail, you reach the climax forest. Brilliant green, vibrant, and healthy, this is the final succession in a series of forest replacements. Full in their foliage, the underbellies of their leaves seem to reflect sunlight downward, creating a glow that provides inspiration and satisfaction.

Proceeding to the end of the trail, you will intersect with MI 93. From here you can turn north and travel through thick forest, or turn south going past the park entrance and heading back to I-75.

5

St. Ignace to Cheboygan

Straits of Mackinac, Colonial Michilimackinac,
Historic Mill Creek

General description: From St. Ignace, which is in the upper peninsula at the entrance to the Mackinac Bridge, you will be following a 25-mile path of Michigan history. This drive to Cheboygan, in the lower peninsula, spans the Straits of Mackinac, a waterway separating the two peninsulas, and visits Colonial Michilimackinac and Historic Mill Creek. You will pass Mackinac Island, location of Fort Mackinac and Mackinac Island State Park. As you follow the northeastern edge of the lower peninsula almost 20 miles to the quaint town of Cheboygan, you will be treated to old pines and views of the Straits of Mackinac.

Special attractions: Mackinac Bridge, Fort Michilimackinac, Mackinaw Maritime Park, Historic Mill Creek, Cheboygan County Historical Museum, Cheboygan Opera House, bird marsh.

Location: Begins in the southern portion of the upper peninsula and travels to the northern portion of the lower peninsula.

Drive route numbers: Interstate 75, US 23, US 2.

Travel season: Year-round. Note that the Cheboygan County Historical Museum and the Cheboygan Opera House are open summer weekday afternoons only. Both charge a small fee.

Camping: Many private campgrounds along the drive, most with rustic cabins.

Services: Food, shopping, hotels in St. Ignace, Mackinac Island, Mackinaw City, and Cheboygan.

Nearby attractions: Mackinac Island, Cheboygan State Park, Bois Blanc Island, Wilderness State Park.

 The drive

Depart St. Ignace on I-75, proceeding south—it can be reached by US 2 from the southern coast of the upper peninsula, or access it from midtown. As your near the southern edge of the upper peninsula, you will see the Mackinac Bridge, or "Mighty Mac," spreading before you. This 5-mile suspension bridge connects the two portions of Michigan by spanning the Straits of Mackinac. Built in 1957, this bridge is the longest of its type in the

Drive 5: St. Ignace to Cheboygan

Straits of Mackinac, Colonial Michilimackinac, Historic Mill Creek

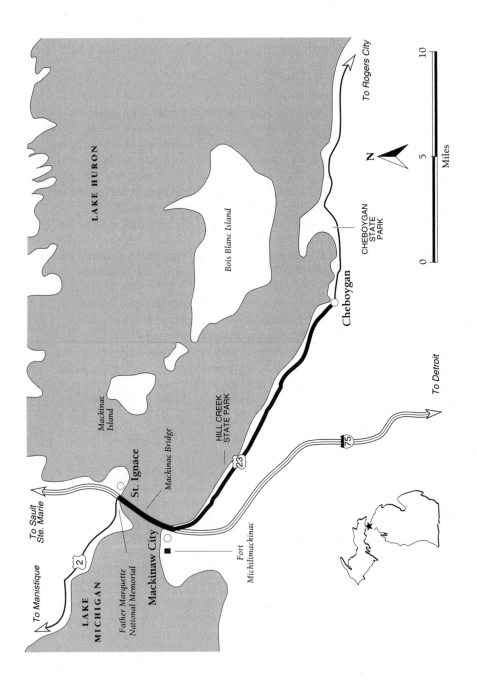

world. It holds a 4-lane road and is 900 feet longer than San Francisco's Golden Gate Bridge. Majestic by day, enchanting at night when fully lit, this bridge has 34 water piers and 2 towers, which rise 552 feet above the tempestuous waters of Lake Michigan to your right (west) and Lake Huron to your left (east).

The Mackinac Bridge is more than a decoration. This bridge became a vital link between the two peninsulas of Michigan because it allowed for quick travel never before possible. This fueled tourism and created economic growth, which has been especially important for the upper peninsula. Prior to 1957, several large ferry boats transported passengers and vehicles across the Straits. This took hours, rather than the minutes it now takes to cross the beautiful bridge.

Midway between peninsulas you may feel awestruck by the strength and grandeur of the bridge itself, accentuated by the crashing waters below. Coasting along, you will also be treated to views of Mackinac Island to your left.

Mackinac Island is a unique community. No motorized vehicles are allowed on the island; travel is by bike, foot, or horse-drawn carriage. Known as a vacation spot for the wealthy since the late 1800s, the island is brimming with beauty and peace. There is an 8-mile path that follows the perimeter of the island. Filled with stately Victorian homes, turn-of-the-century bed and breakfast spots, pricey gift shops, and restaurants, as well as some of the best fudge anywhere, Mackinac Island caters to resorters. The island is home to Fort Mackinac and Mackinac Island State Park.

From 1875 to 1895, the area now known as Mackinac Island State Park was known as Michigan National Park, named so by the United States Congress. It was the nation's second national park. In 1895, the secretary of war signed the park over to the State of Michigan. Today the park encompasses eighty percent of the island.

Fort Mackinac was built on the island when Colonial Michilimackinac, situated in Mackinaw City and under British control, was deemed too vulnerable to American attack. The British abandoned Colonial Michilimackinac in 1779.

For almost fifteen years the British had control of the fort, but in 1796, the Americans gained control by treaty. During the War of 1812, the British recaptured the fort, only to have the Americans reclaim it three years later with another treaty. The Americans controlled the fort until 1895, when it became a state park. The fort grounds include some of Michigan's oldest standing buildings as well as exhibits and interpretative programs. You can catch a ferry to Mackinac Island almost any time of day from St. Ignace or Mackinaw City.

Continuing along the bridge, you have ample opportunity to spot

"Mighty Mac," the Mackinac Bridge, spans the Straits of Mackinac to connect Michigan's upper and lower peninsulas.

activity in the waters below. You may even catch a freighter pushing through the deep blue waters. Passing through the silver arches, you begin a slow descent to the apron of historic Mackinaw City.

This city is rich in history and beauty. One of the first things you may notice in the area are two different spellings of the city's name. Though Mackinac and Mackinaw are pronounced identically, the difference in spelling comes from the history of mixed languages brought to the area by the Ojibwe Indians, the French, and the English. The indians who inhabited this area called it *Michinnimakinong, Mich* for great, *inni* for connecting sound, *maki* for fault, and *nong* for land. The French arrived in 1715, and brought with them the "ac" spelling at the end of the word. The British then changed the end spelling to "aw," though the pronunciation was the same.

Upon entering town, you will see signs directing you to Fort Michilimackinac. Established in 1715 by the French, this restored fort is filled with palisades, lookouts, trails, and homesteads to give you a glimpse of the past. Initially controlled by the French, the British took over the fort in 1761. The Ojibwe who inhabited the region were allies with the French, and became nervous about the change in power. This led to Chief Pontiac's War of 1763.

This clever assault occurred one day as the Ojibwe engaged in a game similar to lacrosse, called *baggatiway*. They played the game at the front gate of the fort, inviting all of the British officers to watch as the players volleyed the ball. One of the lobs vaulted the ball over the gate. The Ojibwe asked permission to enter the fort to retrieve the ball. They repeated this ploy a couple of times, and the third time the players, after grabbing their weapons from beneath their women's skirts, stormed the fort and massacred the British. At the restored fort, you can see live exhibitions and reenactments of this war, and visit a commanding officer's house, a British trader's house, and the Church of St. Anne.

Across the highway from the fort is the Mackinac Maritime Park, home to a replica of the *Welcome*, a boat used to move construction materials from the fort to Mackinac Island, Old Mackinac Point Lighthouse, and the boating museum.

Once back on I-75 South, take exit 38 to get on US 23 to Cheboygan. US 23 is part of the Lake Huron Circle Tour, a self-guided auto route along the shores of Lake Huron. When you reach the four-way stop, approximately 1.5 miles south, where MI 108 intersects with US 23 South, continue south on US 23. From Mackinaw City, it is a fast 14 miles to Cheboygan.

Just outside Mackinaw City, the double lane, narrow highway is heavy with pine and cedar trees. The cedar on your left is tucked between stands

Old buoy at Mackinaw Maritime Park in Mackinaw City.

of old hardwood trees, with cabins, resorts, and small motels allowing for brief openings in the thick forest. Only occasionally can you see the blue waters of Lake Huron on your left.

The brilliant yellow flowers you may see along the side of the road in late spring and early summer have five petals, and appear wet and shiny. One of the most ancient flowers to exist, these buttercups are survivors of the early Cenozoic era. The leaves are good food for ruffed grouse chicks, so keep your eyes open for these birds wherever you see buttercups.

Three miles out of Mackinaw City you will see the entrance to Mill Creek State Park to your right. Historic Mill Creek joined the Mackinac Historic State Parks in 1975 and holds an example of Michigan industry in the 1700s.

This 625-acre nature preserve sits on the shores of mighty Lake Huron. In 1972, archeologists excavated items that revealed this as the former site of a water-powered mill which had produced lumber and grain for the fort at Mackinac Island. The original Mill Creek was constructed by Scotsman Robert Campbell in the 1780s. Archaeologists' excavation of artifacts as well as research of historic documents, provided the basis for reconstruction of this mill. The park also includes a museum and small auditorium.

As you leave the parking lot, turn right onto US 23 to continue south to Cheboygan. You will be traveling through an area of healthy forest, making it possible to sight wild turkey, ruffed grouse, and duck.

At the end of the drive, you enter Cheboygan, a quaint town that is home to three lighthouses. The Cheboygan Light, built in 1853, is located on Lighthouse Point. The Po Reef Light was built in 1929, and the Fourteen Foot Shoal Light marks the shallow shoal-lined area near Cheboygan Harbor's entrance. Cheboygan is the home port for the Coast Guard cutter *Mackinaw*. Specially constructed for rescue, towing, and icebreaking, it is credited with extending the Great Lakes shipping season by six weeks. When the cutter is in port, visitors are welcomed on board for a tour.

Cheboygan also contains one of the Great Lakes' largest cattail marshes, a nesting site for fifty-four bird species. The marsh can be viewed from a boardwalk in Gordon Turner Park at the end of Huron Street, one of the main streets in town, and easy to find. The boardwalk is also a good place to gaze again across the Straits at the Mackinac Bridge, as well as to view Round and Bois Blanc islands.

Before leaving Cheboygan you might also want to visit The Cheboygan County Historical Museum at 404 South Huron Street, and the Opera House at 403 North Huron Street. The museum, a two-story brick structure built in 1882 with attached county jail, served as the town sheriff's home until 1969. The parlor, kitchen, and bedroom have been recreated in period style. The adjoining jail cells contain lumbering, farming, and military exhibits and displays of women's clothing. There is a also nineteenth-century furnished log cabin on the grounds.

The Victorian Opera House was built in 1877, then rebuilt in 1888 following a fire. Mary Pickford, Annie Oakley, and Mademoiselle Rhea were among the theater's actors. The opera house is still a focal point for local entertainment.

Drive 6: Sault Ste. Marie to Whitefish Point

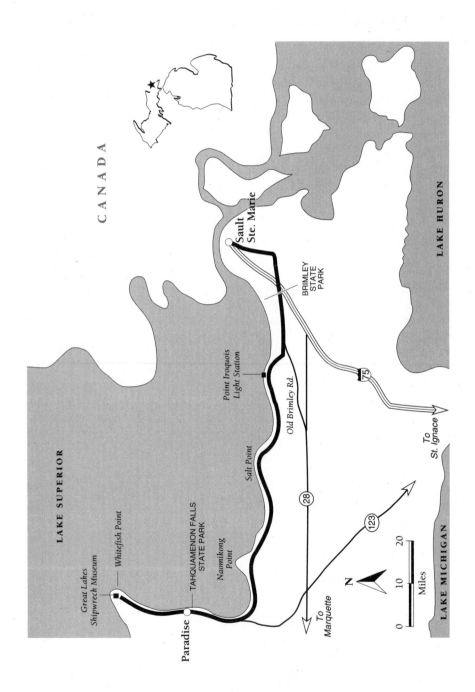

6

Sault Ste. Marie to Whitefish Point

General description: Sault Ste. Marie, the state's oldest city and home of the world famous Soo Locks, is the starting point for this drive, approximately 70 miles. From Sault Ste. Marie, you will follow some of Lake Superior's most beautiful shoreline to the Point Iroquois Light Station. The drives ends at Whitefish Point, home to the Great Lakes Shipwreck Museum and Whitefish Point Bird Observatory.

Special attractions: Bay Mills, Brimley State Park, Point Iroquois Light Station, Whitefish Bay, Paradise, Whitefish Point Bird Observatory, and Great Lakes Shipwreck Museum.

Location: The northeastern area of the upper peninsula.

Drive route numbers: Interstate Business 75, Interstate 75, and County Highway H63.

Travel season: Year-round.

Campground: Two private campgrounds in Sault Ste. Marie, Bay Mills Campground, Monocle Lake, Bay View, Andrus Lake, and Shelldrake Dam.

Services: Very few along drive route. Full services in Sault Ste. Marie. Paradise offers a bakery, grocery store, gas station, and a couple of cafes.

Nearby attractions: Soo Locks Boat Tours, Tower of History, Tahquamenon Falls State Park, and Agawa Canyon.

The drive

Sault Ste. Marie means the "Rapids of St. Mary." Missionaries Isaac Jogues and Charles Raymbault first came to this area in 1641. In 1668 Father Jacques Marquette arrived with Claude Dabon, and together established the very first mission. This area is considered the third oldest establishment in the United States.

Settlement of the northwest territory created a tremendous increase in trade with more large boats needing to pass through this area. The only waterway connecting Lake Superior to the other Great Lakes is the St. Mary's River, which contains St. Mary's Rapids, a fleeting portion of rushing water that falls over 20 feet from Lake Superior to Lake Huron. The rapids made quite a barrier for those hoping to navigate this waterway back in the 1700s. Pioneers had to unload their boats and haul their wares around the rapids only to reload at the other side. A solution was needed for a safe passageway for ships to journey past the powerful St. Mary's Rapids.

In 1797, the Northwest Fur Company built a 38-foot lock for the Canada side of the river. This lock was used primarily for small boats and was destoyed in the War of 1812. In 1852, Congress passed an act granting 750,000 acres of public land to the State of Michigan.

By 1853, the Fairbanks Scale Company, interested in mining opportunites available in the upper peninsula, began to construct the locks for the St. Mary's Rapids. They built tandem locks, each 350 feet long, which work by elevating the water level to a point where a vessel is raised or lowered to the level of the connecting waterway. In 1855, the locks were designated as state locks. There was a toll of four cents per ton for all boats passing through the locks. By 1877 the toll was reduced to three cents.

As commerce and trade increased the locks bustled with activity. It was evident that new locks would soon be needed to accommodate the growing area. However, the state could not afford them. So in 1881, the locks were transferred to United States government ownership, coming under the jurisdiction of the U. S. Army Corps of Engineers. Since that time the Corps has operated and maintained the locks with no toll.

There are three locks presently operating. The MacArthur Lock was named after General Douglas MacArthur. It was constructed in 1943 and is 800 feet long and 80 feet wide. The Poe Lock, namesake of Colonel Orlando M. Poe, Engineer Officer during the Civil War, was contructed in 1968 at a length of 1,200 feet and a width of 110 feet. The Davis Lock, named for

The Great Lakes Shipwreck Museum and Historical Society at Whitefish Point.

Colonel Charles Davis, was constructed in 1914. It is 1,350 feet in length and 80 feet in width.

Sault Ste. Marie is a tourism town that offers many different attractions, most based on the natural resources that bless this area. You can take boat tours of the locks and surrounding areas or explore the SS *Valley Camp* Museum Ship, a steam-powered freighter with exhibits, aquarium, and theaters. St. Mary's River is a fine trout fishing water, and the rapids offer up rainbow trout, whitefish, and Coho Salmon. Fishing here is best the last week of May through mid-June. Sault Ste. Marie, Michigan is connected to Sault Ste. Marie, Ontario by the 2.8-mile-long International Bridge.

You begin this drive in Sault Ste. Marie on I-75 (Business) SW. It eventually turns into CR H63. Follow CR H63 to Six Mile Road. Turn right.

Traveling due west on Six Mile Road, the first several miles are large open farm areas. This area is not necessarily scenic, but interesting all the same. It is not until you have driven about 17 miles that you come to Brimley State Park, situated on the shore of the St. Mary's River. Established in 1923, this park is one of the upper peninsula's oldest and most scenic. Within these 38 acres there are over 250 campsites and a long, wonderful velvety beach to linger on. There is a hiking trail and boat launch as well.

Turn right into the parking lot of Brimley State Park. Headquarters are immediately to your right. Pick up information about the park services and surrounding area here.

Departing the park, turn right onto Six Mile Road which turns into Lakeshore Drive. This portion of the road rounds Waiska bay, on your right. After about 4.5 miles, you pass near the Ojibwe community of Bay Mills. Continue to follow the shoreline as it traces Lake Superior north toward Whitefish Point.

Almost 2 miles past Bay Mills you will pass South Pond on your left. Proceeding along the shore, you soon come to Spectacle Lake on your left, followed by its larger neighbor, Monocle Lake. Here, you will also find the Hiawatha National Forest Recreation Center. This area provides lovely picnic areas and long, deep beaches of soft sand. All summer long you would probably find sunbathers and swimmers enjoying the lapping waves. A beautiful hill of hardwood trees stand to the west. This blend of maple, beech, and birch trees is brilliant in autumn.

Continuing on Lakeshore Drive, head straight for 1 mile until you come to Point Iroquois Light Station. At Point Iroquois Light Station and Museum you will notice a beach dappled with driftwood and colored stones. The 65-foot Point Iroquois Light Station was used for 107 years to warn ships of the slim fit through Point Iroquois and the rocky reef of Canada's Gros Cap. The original wooden structure was built in 1857, but was replaced in 1870 by the brick tower you now see.

The next 5 miles pass through a dense birch-maple-beech forest dotted with only a handful of homes. Lake Superior's Whitefish Bay is on your right.

Six miles past the Point Iroquois Light Station you come to the intersection of Ranger Road and Lake Shore Drive. Continue west by proceeding straight. The road now becomes Lewis Memorial Highway. Two miles past that intersection, you come to Bay View campground to your right. The road etches a portion of shore called Pendills Bay, which is a cozy hamlet tucked into the larger bay of Whitefish.

As the road continues west it yields to hardwood trees. Soon, you cross Pendills Creek, a small stream that empties into the bay. This is a good spot to see yellow-eyed grass, gentle blue forget-me-nots, and spotted knapweed, a pink thistle-like wildflower that thrives in moist conditions.

From this point, the road gently curves to the north for a short distance. There are long, sandy shallow beaches to your right. Several miles later the road intersects with US 123. Turn right and proceed north toward Whitefish point.

The next 7 miles skirt north through a bog area. Here, you will see still pools reflecting back into the sky the outline of nearby shrubs and trees. Lily pads, cattails, and bulrushes form the outer edges of these ponds, creating hiding places for small wildlife. Drive with care—animals often dart out of the protection of the forests laced with buttercups, black spruce, and tamarack trees.

In another mile, you will come to Tahquamenon Falls State Park, Rivermouth Unit, on your right. Based at the point where the Tahquamenon River pours into Lake Superior, this park offers fine hiking and camping as well as cross-country skiing in the winter.

Continue north along Lake Superior. To the left is a heavily wooded area. You continue along the shore of Whitefish Bay to your right, with an open, pristine bog area to your left. It is about 8 miles to the laid-back resort town of Paradise.

Paradise was established in 1925. This small town offers a few conveniences like groceries and gas. Although it is considered a tourist hotspot, it seems to have stayed away from being overdeveloped into a glitzy, fast-paced vacation wonderland. This area is heralded for its abundance of blueberries. The great fire of 1922 destoyed the forest in this area, but it created a habitat ideal for blueberries. Every August a blueberry festival is held here.

It is about 12 miles from Paradise to Whitefish Point. The road is mixed with thick forest and dense wetlands as it creeps toward Whitefish. As you enter the large parking area of Whitefish Point, you will notice several buildings situated on a shore graced with round smooth stones. As you can see, the wooden breakers here have been overwhelmed by the power of the waves. The original lighthouse on this spot was Lake Superior's first, built in 1849.

In the 80-mile area of Whitefish Point, there have been more than 300 shipwrecks and 320 sailors lost. Most notable were the 1816 sinking of the

Point Iroquois Light Station on the shore of Lake Superior.

Invincible and the more recent wreck of the *Edmund Fitzgerald*, which sank in 1975. In 1985, this became the home of the Great Lakes Shipwreck Museum. The museum contains haunting artifacts and model boats such as the schooner *Niagara*. During the mining boom, there was a lot of congestion on the lakes. The 1800s was a time when more than 3,000 vessels competed for space on the waterways, compared to the meager 120 that pass through now. Combine the large numbers with natural elements such as more than 200 miles of open water being roiled up by high winds, fog, or snow, and you can visualize the tumultuous conditions that were created.

Sometimes a shipwreck would occur because a boat ran ashore or was caught upon rocks within shallow areas. Many ships of that time burned wood for their power, so they tried to travel as close to shore as possible in order to be close to their supply of wood.

You will also find the Whitefish Point Bird Observatory here. Located in a small white building that resembles the rest of the structures on the point, it was established in 1978 to study birds of the Great Lakes, focusing on migration habits. This is a fine spot for birders because the land and water nearby form a natural corridor, which directs the birds through the point during migration. This is also a good spot for catching glimpses of red-throated loons and red-necked grebes. Spring migration starts in late March; fall migration starts in late July and continues into November.

Drive 7: Newberry to Tahquamenon Falls

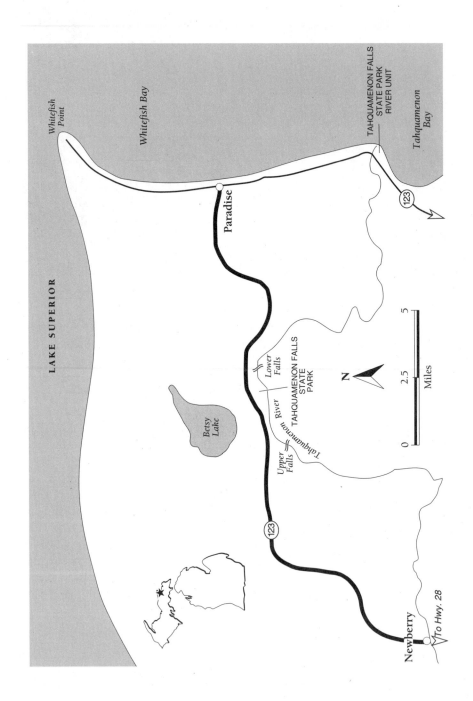

7

Newberry to Tahquamenon Falls

General description: This 43-mile drive from Newberry to Tahquamenon Falls State Park escorts you through thick, moist forest to the second largest waterfall east of the Mississippi.

Special attractions: Tahquamenon Falls State Park, Upper and Lower Falls, North Country Scenic Trail, Giant Pine Hiking Loop.

Location: The east-central portion of the upper peninsula.

Drive route numbers: Michigan Highway 123.

Travel season: Year-round, but almost too busy midsummer.

Camping: Riverbend Campground, Overlook Campground, and nearby Rivermouth Campground.

Services: Some small cafes and motels in Newberry; Upper and Lower Falls have burger places at the visitor centers.

Nearby attractions: St. Ignace, Pictured Rocks National Lakeshore, Sault St. Marie, Soo Locks.

 ## The drive

Begin this drive in Newberry, a charming small town founded in 1882. From Newberry, take MI 123 north. After 2 miles, you will enter the Lake Superior State Forest, thick with white pine and cedar trees.

Four miles farther, a grove of pine trees stands to your left, stately in any season, but especially majestic in winter after fresh dustings of snow. When you have driven about 4.5 miles the road will veer northeast, and then after about another 4.5 miles you will begin traveling due north. Another 4 miles takes you into a marsh area, characterized by gradual openings and closings of mixed forest boundaries. This mixed forest contains black spruce and tamarack trees, as well as northern white cedar. Bogs like this typically harbor acidic waters and lack oxygen, so that many forms of wildlife, such as fish, cannot survive.

About four miles out of the marsh area, you will come to Lake Superior State Forest. The ditches here are lined with lichens and moss, creating a light green and faint blue textured look. These lichens are a combination of algae and fungi, and can survive in numerous conditions. Cracked shield lichen or *Parmelia sulcata*, has many rootlike vestiges that attach to a tree trunk or deep roadside areas. These lichens are flat and dull at first appearance, but if you look closely, you will find an intricate, frilly interior.

In 10 miles more (37 miles from Newberry), you reach the entrance to

The mighty roar of the Upper Falls in Tahquamenon Falls State Park.

Tahquamenon Falls on your right. Tahquamenon Falls State Park is the second largest state park in Michigan. It has more than 35,000 acres of thick forest and lowland area. The water of the Tahquamenon River is quite brown, due to the large amount of tannic acid that is leached from the tamarack and cedar trees that live near the water's edge.

The Upper Falls at Tahquamenon are substantial, roaring and echoing throughout the park. They are 200 feet across and move more than 50,000 gallons of water per second. The drop from the falls into the canyon is more than 48 feet. These falls are actually the second largest next to Niagara Falls. At the park, there are several nice viewing platforms, or you may want to walk to the gentle serene portion of the river. There is a visitor center here, called Camp 33, an interesting log building built without nails. The building houses a gift shop filled with souvenirs and books about the area. Just outside of Camp 33, you will find a picnic area and restaurant. Similar to the layout of old logging camps, the buildings, and tables and chairs are set snugly around a fireplace.

The habitat here is perfect for spotting birds such as gray jays, boreal chickadees, and Connecticut warblers. The area between the Upper and Lower falls is filled with American beech and sugar maple, as well as virgin hemlock and cedar trees. There are river otter here, splashing from shore to river, scampering along the sand-packed banks. In May and July the deer flies, black flies, and mosquitoes are thick.

You can hike from the Upper Falls to the river mouth by taking a portion of the North Country Scenic Trail. The complete trail is more than 200 miles long from Marquette through the Pictured Rocks National Lakeshore and Muskallonge State Park, and passes the falls. When the trail is complete, it will stretch from the Appalachian Trail in New York State to North Dakota. The Upper Falls also has the Giant Pine Loop, which is a 4-mile loop hike through a thick stand of white pine trees.

To reach the Lower Falls, exit the Upper Falls parking lot and turn right (north) on MI 123. Proceed 6 miles downstream to the entrance of the Lower Falls, and turn right into the parking area. You will see a sign directing you to a boardwalk. This is a delightful walkway which pokes through the forest along the river's edge with the smell of wet cedar and pine trees all around, and the roar of the falls beckoning. There is a great gift shop and restaurant at the head of the boardwalk. A foot path winds next to the falls, taking you close to the rumbling water, which drops a mighty 22 feet into a formation created by island rocks and boulders. Here, again, the water looks like the head of a root-beer float—brown and foamy.

This is an extremely popular tourist destination during peak summer months, particularly July and August. It can be a frustrating experience if you are not prepared for heavy traffic, congested parking lots, and busy concession stands. Spring and fall, however, can be delightful times to visit, and for the hearty souls, winter can be breathtakingly beautiful as heavy white snows drape the boughs of sturdy white pine and cedar trees.

The boardwalk at the Lower Falls winds through thick cedar and pine trees.

Drive 8: Grand Marais To Munising

Grand Sable Dunes at Pictured Rocks National Lakeshore

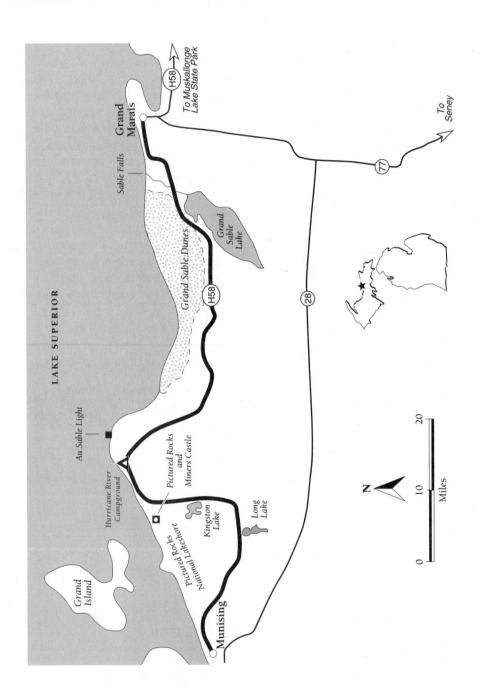

8

Grand Marais To Munising

Grand Sable Dunes at Pictured Rocks National Lakeshore

General description: This drive through the Pictured Rocks National Lakeshore and Grand Sable Bank and Dunes takes you through mammoth dunes and rolling hills situated on the shore of Lake Superior. From Grand Marais to Munising, the 58-mile drive takes you on a narrow, winding, dirt road that rises and falls with steep elevations.

Special attractions: Grand Sable Bank and Dunes, Log Slide, Grand Lake, Pictured Rocks National Lakeshore, Grand Marais Light, Agate Beach, Grand Sable Falls, Au Sable Point and Light, Miners Castle and Falls, Lakeshore Trail, Munising Falls and Rear Range Light, and the Old Sand Point Marsh Trail.

Location: The northeastern coast of the upper peninsula.

Drive route numbers: County Highway H58, Michigan Highway 77, Pictured Rocks National Lakeshore Road, Kingston Lake Road, Adams Trail, Buck Hill Road, Miners Castle Road, Lakeshore Trail, Michigan Highway 28, Washington Street, and Sand Point Road.

Travel season: Most of these roads are not plowed in the winter, so it is generally impossible to travel this route after the first snowfall.

Camping: Grand Marais, Hurricane River Campground, Twelvemile Beach and Campground. Campsites are available along Lakeshore Trail with permit, and there are several private campgrounds in Munising.

Services: Food and lodging in Grand Marais and Munising.

Nearby attractions: Pictured Rocks Boat Tours in Munising, Grand Island.

 The drive

The dirt road along this drive is narrow, old, and bumpy. Although there are a few smooth spots, the road yields to many ruts and grooves, worse in wet weather. It is best explored when you have time to stop and visit the scenic and historical sights.

Grand Marais is perched upon a hilly shore with a bird's-eye view of Lake Superior. This tiny village, tucked into a petite, secure harbor called West Bay, was founded by early French explorers who called it *grand marais*, which means "big marsh."

In the latter portion of the nineteenth century, this was a busy lumber town. In the early 1900s, the lumber industry came to a halt, and the town came to an economic standstill. It was only about fifty years ago that an economic resurgence based on tourism occured. With a population of about four hundred year-round residents, Grand Marais's population triples during summer months. But with miles of picturesque trails and scenic views, this is a hub for snowmobile activity, attracting winter visitors, too.

Pictured Rocks National Lakeshore is 43 miles of shoreline between Grand Marais and Munising to the west. Designated in 1966 as the first national lakeshore in the United States, it is comprised of layers of copper, iron, and other deposits. The deposits create a colorful layer which stands out as the sun sets upon the face of the shore. Copper, with its blue-green hue, and iron, with its reddish tint, blend into a wide harmonious mural. The actual cliffs can be seen only by boat. Boat tours are offered and begin in Munising.

Pictured Rocks National Lakeshore Road is not snowplowed, so this drive is only accessible spring, summer, and fall. The autumn colors in the hardwood trees make this a superb autumn drive.

The drive starts on CR H58, which you can access in Grand Marais by following MI 77 up from the south, or CR H55 from the east. Once on CR

Overlooking Au Sable Lake in the Grand Sable Dunes at Grand Marais.

H58 heading west, follow it through Grand Marais along the shore of West Bay.

After 0.5 mile, the Grand Marais Light and a stone fishing pier are to your right. You will also see Grand Marais Beach, a fine swimming area. You can walk the beach about 0.5 mile west until it blends into an area called Agate Beach. Agate Beach is, just as the name implies, a place where you can find Lake Superior agates, characterized by their stripes. These banded agates are formed when liquid quartz adheres inside the cavities of rocks that have become porous over the years. Different colors occur due to varied impurities in the quartz.

Proceed west for 1 mile on CR H58 out of Grand Marais. You will pass the Grand Sable Falls to your right. There is a parking lot and short trail to the falls, obviously marked. Your best view of the falls is obtained if you take the short walk and follow the staircase that leads right to the edge of the cascading water.

Continue west on CR H58 until it makes a sharp turn to the left after about 0.25 mile. Here, turn right on Kingston Lake Road.

Proceed 1 mile and Grand Sable Lake will appear to your left amid wide, mammoth dunes. Located to your right is the doorstep to the Grand Sable Dunes. Grand Sable Bank and Dunes sprawl for almost 5 miles and amass a height of 275 feet. Bleak, bare, yet naturally stunning, they have little vegetation. The sand moves with the wind, which creates subtle and gentle formations upon the faces of the dunes. There are accents of marram grass which provide a sparse cover for the upland sandpiper. The upland sandpiper, or "grass plover" as hunters sometimes call it, breeds in open places like this. A thin bird with wiry, yellowish legs, the upland sandpiper is characterized by its long, slender neck and small head and bill. Brownish colored with a white streak underneath, these birds were hunted voraciously at one time and faced near depletion. Their numbers are now steadily increasing.

There are several points where you can stop and explore the dunes. The area is well-marked, and magnificent views can be found from many points.

The road dips away from the shore after about 6 miles, exposing pockets of dense hardwood trees to your left and right. In 2 more miles you come to an area known as the log slide. This slide was in use in the 1800s, when loggers careened raw timber down to lumber schooners waiting to carry it away. The descent is almost 500 feet.

Ten miles into it, the road takes you near the shore again at Hurricane River Campground, to your right. Hurricane River has campsites and great swimming. If you wish to take a short side trip to the Au Sable Point Light and Lighthouse, turn right at the campground and walk the short distance to the site. Au Sable Point Light and Lighthouse contains a lightkeeper's quarters made from sturdy red brick, and a slim white tower, set amid sandstone and crashing Lake Superior waves.

From the campground, head west on CR H58, which is also Kingston Lake Road, along the shoreline. In about 2 miles, you reach Twelvemile Beach and Campground, which greets the crush of Lake Superior waves with a heavily pebbled and somewhat sandy shore. You can access this beach by walking from the parking area through a forest of white birch.

For the next 4 miles the road proceeds south into the hardwood interior of the upper peninsula. A blend of patchy marsh areas and mixed deciduous forest, this portion of the drive is a brilliant fall route, a less thrilling drive in other seasons. In another mile, you will pass Kingston Lake, on your right. Continue as the road sways to the left and right while rolling up and down.

After 6 miles, turn right at Adams Trail, which is also CR H58. Continue west for another mile as the road plunges into the depths of the forest. In 2 miles, Long Lake is to your left. The road continues through hardwood trees, and in another 2 miles, curves sharply to your left proceeding southward. Here, the road becomes Buck Hill Road. There is a dense marsh area to your left, composed of a still pond lined with fir and shrubs. To your right, hills of hardwood trees open to small lakes.

For the next 10 miles the road continues the hills and curves mixed with forest and marsh area. Watch for a sharp right turn at the end of this 10 miles.

For a nice break, turn right after 1 mile onto Miners Castle Road. From the turnoff it is only 6 miles to one of the best views along the Pictured Rocks National Lakeshore. Miners Castle and Falls is a natural rocky structure, resembling a castle, towering nearly nine stories tall. From its vantage point, you can see clear down to the rocky bottom of Lake Superior.

Leaving Miners Castle and Falls from Miners Castle Road, turn right onto CR H58 to proceed west to Munising. In about 5 miles you will come to the trailhead for the Lakeshore Trail, to your right. The Lakeshore Trail is a 43-mile hiking opportunity which follows the national shoreline. It is a "hikers-only" trail, which takes, typically, about three nights and four days to travel. There are some campsites available if you have a permit, which you can get at the Hiawatha National Forest/Pictured Rocks National Lakeshore Visitor Information Center. The Center is located at the intersection of MI 28 and CR H58. (It is open daily from May through October 15 from 9 A.M. to 5 P.M., and to 6 P.M. from mid-June through mid-September. All other months the hours are Monday-Saturday from 9 A.M. to 4:30 P.M.)

Once you arrive in the heart of Munising, about 2.5 miles from Lakeshore Trail, you will see Munising Beach and Munising Bay to your right. The spring-fed Horseshoe Falls can be found to your left in about 0.5 miles.

The sweep of the Au Sable Dunes near Grand Marais.

Continue west 1 mile to the intersection of MI 28 and CR H58 to Munising Falls and Rear Range Light. Turn right into the parking lot. You will find an excellent interpretive center which gives information about the area's geology and history. The falls are especially intense as the water drops 50 feet into a slim, rocky basin.

Also at the intersection of MI 28 and CR H58 is the Old Sand Point Marsh Trail. This is a 0.5 mile walk atop a boardwalk through a 25-acre area of pristine wetland. A backdrop of Lake Superior, jagged cliffs, and sandy dunes provides a well composed picture of geological magic.

This is prime territory for beavers and wetland-related songbirds, so be prepared to catch a glimpse of working wildlife, especially if you are visiting during dusk or dawn. There are sixteen exhibits along the trail to relate the history of the area.

To reach Old Sand Point Marsh Trail, which is barrier-free, follow CR H58 past the intersection of MI 28 and CR H58 to Washington Street. Turn right on Washington. When you have passed the hospital, the road will change to Sand Point Road on which you will continue for 2 miles to the parking area.

Drive 9: Seney National Wildlife Refuge
Marshland Wildlife Drive

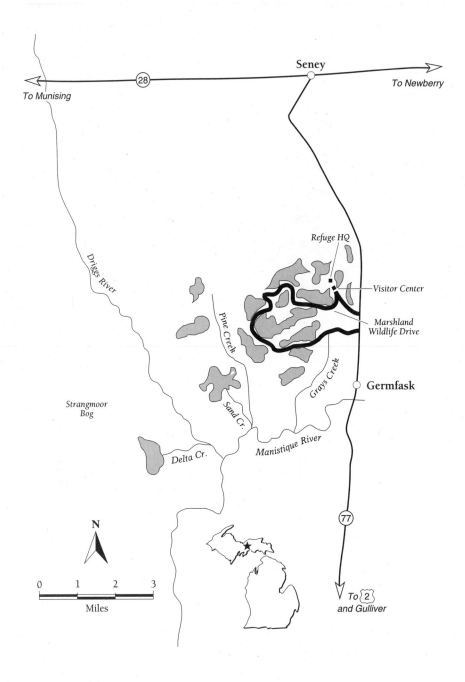

To Munising

28

Seney

To Newberry

Driggs River

Refuge HQ

Visitor Center

Pine Creek

Marshland
Wildlife Drive

Grays Creek

Germfask

Strangmoor
Bog

Sand Cr.

Delta Cr.

Manistique River

N

77

0   1   2   3
Miles

To 2
and Gulliver

9

Seney National Wildlife Refuge
Marshland Wildlife Drive

General description: Seney National Wildlife Refuge is located in the Great Manistique Swamp. The refuge is a mosaic of bulrushes, nesting areas, shag forests, and shore-lingering waterfowl containing more than 95,000 acres of swamp situated in the upper peninsula. This area offers the 7-mile Marshland Wildlife Drive, which takes you through a restored wetland created by a series of manmade dikes. Driving through this national refuge, you are rewarded with close-up views of more than two hundred species of birds and a variety of animals such as beaver, muskrat, and otter. The wetland is composed of 21 artificial pools and 750 islands, all created to aid in the protection of wildlife.

Special attractions: The reflection of a Great Blue Heron walking through a still pool, the flutter of birds, and the splash of animals such as beaver and otter.

Location: The center of the upper peninsula.

Drive route numbers: Michigan Highway 28 and Michigan Highway 77.

Travel season: Closed from October 15 to May 15, but sometimes closes earlier. Call ahead in the late fall.

Camping: The drive itself offers no camping, but there are campsites in Germfask, as well as in Mead Creek Campground, which is 15 miles south of Seney in the Lake Superior Forest.

Services: Best source of food, lodging, and services is in nearby Germfask.

Nearby attractions: Fox River Hiking Trail north of Seney, Manistique Lakes and River.

 # The drive

Located in the Great Manistique Swamp, the Seney National Wildlife Refuge, containing more than 95,000 acres of swamp, bog, and forest, wasn't always a preferred habitat for an abundance of wildlife. Like most of the upper peninsula, this area was obliterated by the logging era of the 1800s. As a method of cleaning up, logging companies started intentional fires. Such a practice often, as in this case, nearly destroys the humus soil. Mischievous developers drained the land and sold pieces of it to farmers, sight unseen. The land was not farmable, and eventually reverted to the state for taxes.

In 1934 the State of Michigan recommended that this area, thought to be a vast wasteland, be developed as a wildlife refuge. In 1935, the area was established as the Seney National Wildlife Refuge. Its goal is the protection of wildlife.

The Civilian Conservation Corps (CCC) built a series of dikes and ditches to impound the water so it would pool in areas and create marshes for the waterfowl and other marsh-seeking wildlife. A marsh is defined as a shallow basin of water that contains shore-to-shore growth of soft-stemmed aquatic plants such as cattails, bulrushes, and water lilies. The CCC and Work Projects Administration (WPA) were also responsible for planting aquatic plants such as bulrushes and duck weed, so the marsh would quickly mimic the cycles of nature. But this marsh does not mimic nature all by itself. The wetlands in the refuge are helped in sustaining an active environment by the raising and lowering of its water levels. This allows any plant life that may be in distress from too much water, the chance to recover and also allows bottom seeds the chance to germinate.

To reach this drive, take MI 28 out of Seney and turn left (south) onto MI 77 to Seney National Wildlife Refuge. The refuge entrance is approximately 4.8 miles from MI 28. The refuge is 3 miles north of Germfask on MI 28. As you approach the refuge, turn right into the entrance. The visitor center, to the right, is a good place to stop for information about the refuge

Entrance to the Seney National Wildlife Refuge.

and its inhabitants. Left of the visitor center is a sign for the self-guided auto tour, called the Marshland Wildlife Drive.

This one-way gravel road is well maintained and well marked with signs designating sharp curves and blind spots. The pools are marked by letters A through J. Brochures from the information center are helpful, too. There are three observation decks along the drive; feel free to stop and peek—the telescopes provided are free. Drive slowly and carefully, and watch for wildlife so you will not disturb them.

After the first mile, the road is briefly two-way traffic. You are driving next to pool F on your right. Take the first left at 1 mile into the drive. There will be a sign instructing you that the road has now become one-way.

You begin to see the emerging blend of bogs and marsh that comprise the refuge. A flutter of birds, a scurry of wings, and your arrival at the marsh has been announced. To your left is pool C, and to your right is pool E. Pool E, one of the larger pools in the refuge, is a good spot for watching loons. The common loon is distinguished by black and white markings, and a distinct soulful wail. The male common loons arrive at the refuge in May, ahead of the females. When the females arrive, a brief courtship occurs and nests are built near the edges of the marsh. The female loon typically lays a pair of eggs, and both parents assume incubation duty. Chicks hatch mid-June, and are frequently seen riding on the backs of their parents. The down-covered babies do this to protect themselves from getting soaked, which could ultimately lead to death from exposure. Eventually, they are led by their parents to a "nursery"—a quiet, shallow cove—where they are taught to swim, fish, and dive.

Memorial Day through mid-July is a critical time for nesting loons, during which they must not be disturbed. Loon nests are typically found at the water's edge, or within 15 feet of water. A loon nest is made of vegetation placed in small piles out the way of the wind. Any type of threat will send a loon scurrying from its nest into the water.

As you will see from Pool E to your right and C to your left, the waters of these marshes are golden brown, due to a high content of tannic acid and other matter. You can also see reddish brown tints in the water from the iron and algae which have concentrated in spots and settled to the botton, creating layers of "bog iron."

Canada geese, trumpeter swans, and sandhill cranes are prominent residents at the marsh. Young ducklings often hide among the bulrushes. Bulrushes are an important contributors to this ecosystem. Not only do bulrushes, 2- to 10-feet tall with rusty, seed-like spearheads, propagate in the shallows of marshes and bogs, but they provide protection and food for waterfowl. The bulrushes also slow harsh waves, which could possibly damage the dikes.

You will also notice many dead trees poking up from the water. These are referred to as "snags." These barren, gnarly-looking distressed hollows also have a task here at the refuge. They provide homes and nesting places for many inhabitants such as the colorful and quirky wood duck.

Four miles into the refuge drive, a trailhead for several roads open only to biking can be found. The marsh is a great place for biking and hiking. If you are a hearty walker, there are times of the year that you can hike in to the Strangmoor Bog, a series of finger-like bogs that alternate with sand dunes. It is a unique opportunity to see an environment that typically exists only in arctic or subarctic regions. You can get details about this hike from the visitor center.

As you pass the trailhead you will notice forests to your right and left. Many of the trees here on the refuge are red and jack pines. Able to survive on sandy soil, the red pine is characterized by long needles and red bark growing on a straight trunk. Jack pine has scraggly branches and bark that is nearly black. You will see scars on many of the large red pines. Such scars were created during the fires that were set during the turn of the century to clean up after the logging era and clear the area for farming.

As you head toward the end of the drive, the road takes you straight out to MI 77. From here, you can proceed north to Seney, or turn right and travel south to Germfask.

10

Champion to L'Anse
Van Riper State Park

General description: This 45-mile drive from Champion to L'Anse takes you through Van Riper State Park, release site of a reintroduced moose population in the 1980s. The entire area of this drive cuts through "moose country," an area of moist forests and wetland features preferred by moose. You will also pass several waterfalls as you make your way north to the head of Keweenau Bay on the shore of Lake Superior.

Special attractions: Van Riper State Park, Canyon Falls, Upper Falls, Daults Falls, Falls River Falls, Lower Falls River Falls, and the Falls River. Moose spotting, beautiful forests.

Location: The northwestern upper peninsula.

Drive route numbers: U.S. Highway 41 and Michigan Highway 28.

Travel season: Year-round.

Camping: Limited camping on drive. Private camping areas on Lake Michigamme and in nearby Marquette. Baraga State Park in Baraga, 4 miles west of L'Anse offers campsites.

Services: Food and lodging in Champion and L'Anse.

Nearby attractions: Keweenaw Peninsula, Copper Harbor.

 The drive

There are hundreds of inland lakes in the upper peninsula, more than 150 waterfalls, and a Great Lakes shoreline of 1,100 miles. This moist land creates not only spectacular beauty in the wake of its moving water, but helps sustain an environment which can support herds of moose. This drive begins in "moose country" and takes you through pretty waterfall territory. You will travel west from Champion through Van Riper State Park which is located in the northwestern part of the upper peninsula. Champion is 17 miles northwest of Ishpeming and about 30 miles west of Marquette.

Take US 41, also known as MI 28, west out of Champion. About 1 mile west of Champion is Van Riper State Park, a 1,200-acre park with campground, picnic area, park store, and bathhouse. Turn left into the park entrance, which is clearly marked. At the visitor center you can learn about Moose Lifts I and II. Those were the names given to the replanting of moose from the Algonquin National Park in Ontario, Canada. The lifts occured in

Drive 10: Champion to L'Anse

Van Riper State Park

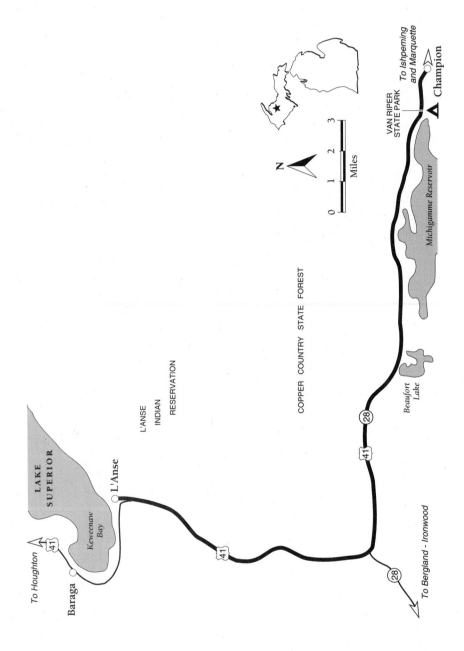

1985 and 1987, when 59 moose were released only 6 miles north of the park. Moose Lifts I and II have proven successful, and as the wooded areas nearby have experienced regrowth over time, the transplanted moose have found a good habitat and reproduced steadily. The center has pictures and video explaining the transplantation, as well as moose artifacts such as racks, fur, and tags.

Prior to the 1880s, moose were abundant in this area. Roaming freely through young tender woods in the winter and lazily nibbling at fresh lily pads in the summer, the population was healthy and strong. However, logging stripped the land and devastated the animals' preferred habitat of bark, twigs, and leafy vegetation. Also contributing to the decrease in population were the mining industry, and the European settlers who hunted the moose for food and hide.

The new habitat, which emerged from the clearing of the land, proved ideal for whitetail deer, and their population soared. The moose population went into serious decline at this point because whitetail deer carry a parasite called brainworm. Harmless to deer, the brainworm is typically fatal to moose. As the deer popluation soared, so did the abundance of brainworm, which invaded many moose and ravaged the herds. Even today, up to thirty percent of Michigan moose die from the brainworm parasite each year.

Moose love to browse on bark and twigs in the winter months, and peruse marshy shallows searching for juicy aquatic plants in the warm summer months. The best time to look for moose is at dawn or dusk. Stream banks, or the open waters above them, are good places from which to observe.

Proceed west out of the state park on US 41. Lake Michigamme is to your left. Noted for its tremendous walleye fishing, this lake has many islands and a rocky, irregular shoreline. After about 6 miles, you will leave Marquette County and enter Baraga County, which was named after Bishop Frederick Baraga. Many early trading posts were developed in this area due to the abundance of fur-bearing animals such as beaver, mink, and fox.

Four miles into Baraga County you drive through an area known as Three Lakes. Beaufort Lake, which also has a campground, is to your left. George Lake, to your left, and Ruth Lake, to your right, follow Beaufort Lake. At this point on the drive you begin to cross many waterways. Rivers and streams abound here. A stream or river is in perpetual motion; a river of any size creates change in the environment it flows through, which in turn changes the river every moment its water passes by.

Another 8 miles takes you across Lateral Creek, and after an additional mile, you will cross the Tioga River. Continue on and proceed over Pelkie Creek and then Hickey Creek, which has a dense marsh area to your right. Look for moose here.

The saga of Operation Mooselift is told at Van Riper State Park.

After 7 more miles you approach Canyon Falls and Upper Falls. Both are to your left. You can turn left into a scenic area for viewing the rushing waters as they spin by.

As you near L'Anse you come to a series of waterfalls created by the Falls River. About 6 miles from Canyon Falls and Upper Falls, Daults Falls will appear to your right. One mile later on the left, the Upper Falls River Falls. You are now only 1.5 miles out of L'Anse.

As you come into town, you will find Falls River Falls to your left, and as you near the Shore of Lake Superior, Lower Falls River Falls will be to your right.

L'Anse, poulation about 2,400, is located at the head of Keweenaw Bay and was the center of the Ford Motor Corporation's upper peninsula enterprises during the 1940s. Today, it is simply a little town on the bay.

11

Gay to Copper Harbor

Keweenaw Peninsula Shore

General description: This 62-mile drive begins in the small town of Gay on the eastern shore of the Keweenaw Peninsula, and follows Scenic Shoreline Drive northeast along the coast of the peninsula, turns inland northwest to Copper Harbor on the peninsula's west edge, and offers short side-trips from Copper Harbor to historic Fort Wilkins and Estivant Pines Nature Area.
Special attractions: Fort Wilkins State Park, Estivant Pines Trail
Location: The northwest portion of the upper peninsula.
Drive route numbers: U.S. Highway 41, Copper City Gay Road.
Travel season: Year-round, but check road conditions during winter.
Camping: Fort Wilkins State Park.
Services: Small restaurants and shops in Copper Harbor.
Nearby attractions: Eagle Harbor, Sand Dunes Drive, Jacobs Falls.

 The drive

You can reach Gay, located on the eastern edge of the Keweenaw Peninsula, by taking US 41 north out of Hancock and proceeding about 12 miles to Copper City Gay Road. Turn right and travel another 12.7 miles into Gay.

Begin this drive in Gay by turning onto the Scenic Shoreline Drive and traveling northeast along the shore. You will notice sandy shoreline capped with heavy pines in spots. The road is narrow and weather-beaten, testimony to the hard weather that stretches out of Lake Superior's fingers.

Five miles up the shoreline on your right, you pass Black Rock Point, a small rocky outcropping. As you continue north, the trees grow thicker and are covered with lichen. Lake Superior provides sweeping views to your right. Notice the bent pines along the banks of Lake Superior, shaped by the lake's strong, persistant winds.

About 2 miles farther, you will cross the Big Betsy River and then come to the town of Betsy along the shore of Betsy Bay. One mile later along the shore, you will pass the Betsy River. At this point, take the road as it veers due north (to your left) and head toward Lac La Belle. As you reach Lac La Belle, you will see Haven Falls, a moderate waterfall.

From Lac La Belle, you can proceed east about 1 mile to the Bete Grise

Drive 11: Gay to Copper Harbor
Keweenaw Peninsula Shore

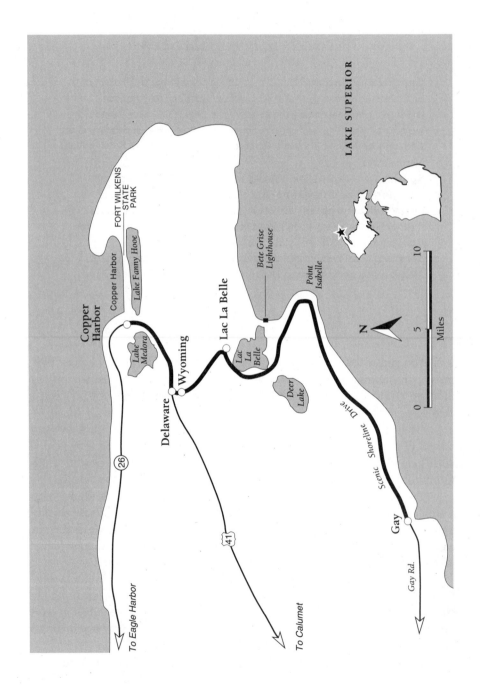

Light by first turning north and then following the road east to the light. You will find a lighthouse and a boat access on Bete Grise Bay which welcomes waters from Lac La Belle. Across the bay is an area called Bear Bluff, a popular nesting spot for eagles. Return to Scenic Shoreline Drive and continue north for another 8 miles to its junction with US 41.

Turn right in Wyoming on US 41 and proceed past Lake Medora to Copper Harbor, another 12 miles. This drive is filled with large, heavy, moss-covered pine trees. The shore is rocky and boasts outcroppings of weather-worn pines. The area around Copper Harbor is American black bear habitat.

As you reach Copper Harbor, several road signs direct you to Fort Wilkins, 2.5 miles east of Copper Harbor on US 41.

In 1843, a schooner searching for a port stopped at the Keweenaw Peninsula. The explorers aboard were the gentlemen who first discovered native copper in the area. From that point on, a mass of people flooded the area. The population increase and copper mining rush led to the building of Fort Wilkins, built by the A and B companies of the Fifth Infantry of Detroit. The greatest concern for the new inhabitants was that friction might erupt between the area's Native Americans and the high-spirited newcomers. By 1846, one-man prospecting gave way to large mining operations. In the 1870s, the army abandoned the fort. Fort Wilkins became a state park in 1923.

From US 41, turn into the fort's parking area. The most noticeable feature here is the large trees blanketed with lichen. The trees yield to a

Exhibit halls at Fort Wilkins State Historical Park near Copper Harbor.

sidewalk leading up to a visitor center and park store.

As you explore Fort Wilkins, which has maintained some of the stuctures of the original fort, you meet interpretive players who delightfully and accurately reconstruct Copper Harbor's past.

From Copper Harbor, you can also take a side trip to Estivant Pines Sanctuary, one of the last remaining stands of virgin white pine trees in Michigan. To reach Estivant Pines from Copper Harbor, travel toward Fort Wilkins State Park and follow the signs to the main parking lot of the sanctuary.

Estivant Pines Sanctuary is administered by the Michigan Nature Association, a private volunteer group. Hiking trails beginning at the parking area allow visitors to walk, hike, or jog on paths through stands of huge trees, some more than five hundred years old. Hike to "Leaning Giant," a mammoth white pine tree estimated to be 120 feet tall. The tree was knocked over during a storm in 1987.

Copper Harbor, a quaint village situated on the shore of Lake Superior, had its first harbor light erected in 1849. The lighthouse that exists now is 100 feet from the site of that original tower. Considered the hotspot for all of Keweenaw County, Copper Harbor, rich in its mining heritage, is a good spot to find handmade gifts such as thimbleberry jam, a favorite made by locals from brightly adorned thimbleberry bushes.

Roadside park near Lac La Belle.

12

Brockway Mountain Drive

General description: This 10-mile drive through Brockway Mountain is often touted as one of the most beautiful drives in Michigan. From its highest point you have an eagle-eye view of Lake Superior and thick, pristine forest hills below.

Special attractions: Hawk migrations, wild orchids.

Location: The northwestern portion of the Keweenaw Peninsula, in the northwestern part of the upper peninsula.

Drive route numbers: Michigan Highway 26, Brockway Mountain Drive.

Travel season: Brockway Mountain Drive is closed after the first snowfall. Call after October 15.

Camping: None on drive.

Services: Full services in Copper Harbor and Eagle Harbor.

Nearby attractions: Fort Wilkins Historic State Park, Estivant Pines Nature Area.

 ## The drive

You start this drive by heading west on MI 26 out of Copper Harbor. Signs direct you to Eagle Harbor. You can continue straight on MI 26, or turn left onto Brockway Mountain Drive. This chapter describes Brockway Mountain Drive; however, it is closed after the season's first snowfall. After turning left onto Brockway Mountain Drive, you will ascend a very narrow, winding hill. On both sides of the road here, thick-needled trees create habitat for much wildlife. This two-lane road is unmarked, and more like a switchback than a road. The road is lined with white posts that mark the sharpest curves. Although it is paved, it has suffered some deterioration, probably due to harsh weather.

At about mile 4, there is a scenic overlook to the right and the left. These pullouts allow room for a couple of cars, and an area to stand and gasp at the great beauty below. The pullouts are marked with gothic stone guardrails, which were created as part of a "make work" project during the Depression.

Look for West Bluff Scenic View at mile 6 of the drive. At this point you are only 10 miles from Eagle Harbor. The elevation here is 735 feet above lake level and 1,337 feet above sea level, making this the highest

Drive 12: Brockway Mountain Drive

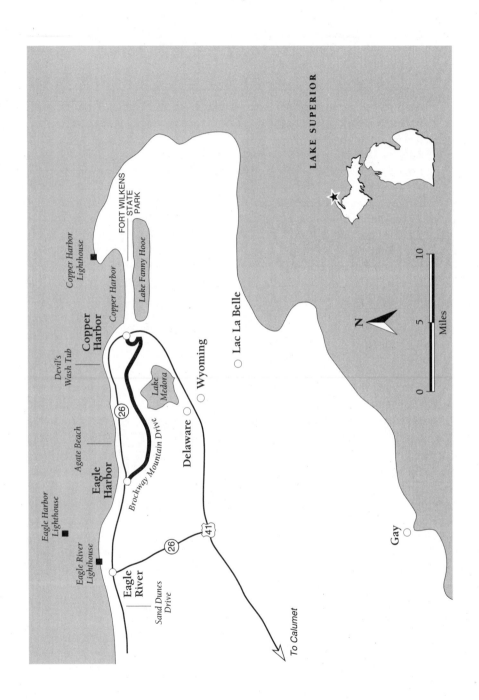

The Eagle Harbor Lighthouse at the end of the Brockway Mountain Drive.

point between the Rocky Mountains and the Allegheny Mountains. The peak of this mountain is a hawk migration path. Hawks migrate northeast along the Keweenaw Peninsula because they can get a good airlift by the updrafts at the end of the peninsula.

This area offers some recreational opportunities such as flower-viewing, rockhounding, birdwatching, and mountain biking. The dense, moist forest here is prime for the growth of orchids. It is best to check with officials at the Copper Country State Forest before picking them to discover if they are state protected. The views along the entire drive are breathtaking. You see rich depths of undisturbed forests covering the hills to your left. This drive is ablaze with changing foliage during autumn, offering one of the most richly colored drives in the area.

After 9 miles into the drive, you join MI 26 again at the Silver River and Silver Falls, and continue to Eagle Harbor.

Eagle Harbor was named for the Eagle Harbor Mining Company, which was based here until 1845. Once you are in Eagle Harbor you will see the Eagle Harbor Rear Range Light to your right, and 0.5 mile down you will see the Eagle Harbor Light. You can take a quick side trip to Eagle River by following the Great Sand Bay south along MI 26 for about 8 miles. This stretch of drive, which has been compared to Scandinavia with its sandy beaches, rocky shores, and thick forest, is called the Sand Dunes Drive and has many pulloffs in case you are tempted to put your feet in the refreshing waters of Lake Superior.

13

Bessemer to Black River Harbor

General description: Designated as a National Scenic Byway, this rolling 15-mile drive from Bessemer to Black River Harbor takes you through roads thick with pine and cedar trees, to an area near Black River Harbor filled with waterfalls created by the Black River.

Special attractions: Algonquin, Great Conglomerate, Rainbow, and Gorge falls, the Black River, and Black River Harbor Recreation Area.

Location: The northwest section of the upper peninsula.

Drive route numbers: North Bessemer Road, U.S. Highway 2, County Road 513 (Black River Road).

Travel season: Year-round, but check with the Michigan Highway Department during times of bad weather or heavy snows.

Camping: Limited camping on drive. Private camping areas on Lake Michigamme and in nearby Marquette. Black River Harbor Campground.

Services: Food and lodging in Bessemer and Black River Harbor.

Nearby attractions: Copper Peak Ski Flying Area, Big Powderhorn Ski Resort, Blackjack Ski Resort, Mount Zion Ski Area, and the city of Ironwood.

 # The drive

The drive between Bessemer and Black River Harbor is designated as a National Scenic Byway because of its pristine forest beauty and abundance of waterfalls. The waterfalls dance, spin, and tumble the water of the Black River through various rock formations all the way to Lake Superior. This road flows freely through stands of pine, hemlock, and hardwood trees.

In 1904, the state built a wagon road from Bessemer to Lake Superior which eventually became known as this drive—the Black River Scenic Byway. However, it was not until 1992 that this area was dedicated as a National Scenic Byway.

As you take this 15-mile drive north from Bessemer, you will be treated to some of the most scenic beauty in the upper peninsula in an area as rich in history as it is rich in thick, fragrant pine and cedar trees. You begin in the small town of Bessemer, named for the inventor who created the Bessemer process for making steel. This town of approximately 2,500 people is

Drive 13: Bessemer to Black River Harbor

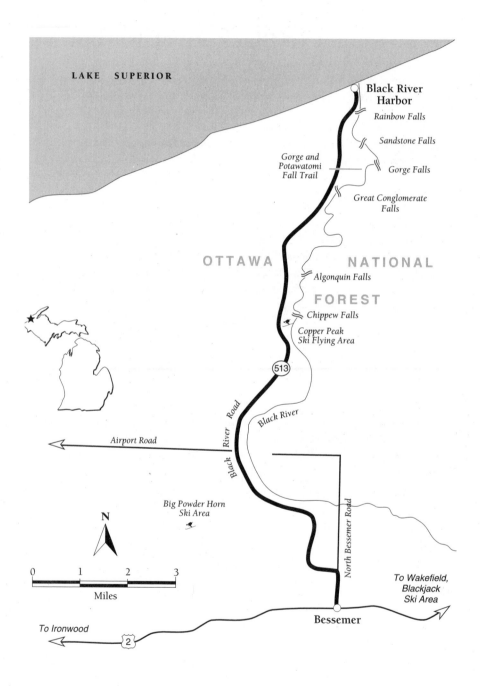

LAKE SUPERIOR

Black River Harbor

Rainbow Falls

Sandstone Falls

Gorge and Potawatomi Fall Trail

Gorge Falls

Great Conglomerate Falls

OTTAWA   NATIONAL

Algonquin Falls

FOREST

Chippew Falls

Copper Peak Ski Flying Area

513

Black River Road

Black River

Airport Road

Big Powder Horn Ski Area

N

0   1   2   3
Miles

North Bessemer Road

To Wakefield, Blackjack Ski Area

Bessemer

To Ironwood

2

located at the intersection of North Bessemer Road and US 2.

Once you are in Bessemer, turn north on CR 513, also known as Black River Road. The road darts westward for about 0.25 mile and then curves sharply to the north. Proceed north on CR 513. After 2 miles you will see Powderhorn Falls to your left. Big Powderhorn, a popular downhill ski resort, is nearby.

As you continue forward along Black River Road, you will travel through hilly terrain filled with pine and cedar trees. Many old growth hardwood and tamarack trees mingle in the mixed forest. After approximately 11 miles, you will arrive at Copper Peak Ski Flying Area and Chippewa Falls, both to your right.

Proceeding north, you come to Algonquin Falls in less than 1 mile. The falls are to your right. The road from this point on is very hilly, loping up and down amid thick trees. Continue north toward Black River Harbor. Just past Copper Peak Ski Flying Hill are the Great Conglomerate Falls, on your right. You can access the falls via a 0.75 mile hiking trail. It is a strenuous walk in parts, and the best advice is to pace yourself.

As you near the edge of the river, the hiking trail will drop considerably, exposing the falls. You will notice how the river separates into two sections, spinning water 40 feet down into an area of conglomerate rock. The surrounding area is filled with old growth hemlock and hardwood trees.

The Gogebic County Courthouse in Bessemer.

Back on CR 513, you immediately come to Gorge Falls, on your right. To reach the falls you can take a hiking trail from the parking lot to a series of stairways and observation platforms. You will be treated to spectacular views of Gorge and Potawatomi Falls. Gorge Falls is almost 30 feet wide and throws water down a distance of more than 24 feet. Potawatomi is 130 feet wide and has a 30 foot drop.

In less than 0.5 mile to the north, you come to Sandstone Falls, on your right. Its riverbed is made of intense red rock, as you might guess. From the parking lot, take the short hike down a stairway to the falls. This is a small waterfall based in a area of varied rock formations carved by the rushing waters.

Back on CR 513, head north a short distance to Rainbow Falls. You can park in the paved lot at Rainbow Falls. A short hiking trail takes you about 0.5 mile to an observation platform which overlooks the Black River and the falls. The name Rainbow Falls came from the rainbow effect sometimes created here when sunlight hits the falling water and creates a mist that seems to be filled with color. In autumn, particularly September, chinook and coho salmon make upstream runs to the falls.

Proceed north 0.5 mile on CR 513 and you will reach Black River Harbor. Black River Harbor, one of only two harbors included within the National Forest System, is a poular recreation spot. Situated at the mouth of

The Rainbow Falls on the Black River.

the Black River, the park consists of three major areas: the harbor and picnic ground, a campground, and the waterfall observation facilities which you have just seen. There is also a boat ramp which is one of Lake Superior's few access points.

It was 1848 when William A. Burt, land surveyor for the United States government, surveyed the area known today as the Black River Recreational Area. A map created by Burt shows a mere wagon road traveling from Black River's mouth to Chippewa Hill. Chippewa Hill is, today, Copper Peak Ski Flying Area. There was also a trail that went from the river's mouth to the Gogebic Range iron mines.

In 1924, Gogebic County bought land for Black River Harbor Park. Upon that action, the residents, mainly fisherman who made their livelihood from the area's trout population, were forced to move. Many of them made new homes in an area now called Black River Village. In 1967, Gogebic County, due to increased management costs, exchanged the area, along with additional potential recreation sites, with the federal government for National Forest Land. Since that time, this area has been under the jurisdiction of the USDA Forest Service.

14

Wakefield to Porcupine Mountain Wilderness State Park

General description: This drive of about 40 miles, from Wakefield to the Porcupine Mountain Wilderness, or "The Porkies" as they are affectionately called, takes you into some of the deepest, most pristine areas of wilderness that exist today.

Special attractions: The unspoiled forests, the waterfalls at the southwest unit of the area, Lake of the Clouds Scenic Overlook.

Location: The northwest portion of the upper peninsula.

Drive route numbers: County Road 519 North, South Boundary Road, Michigan Highway 107.

Travel season: South Boundary Road is not snowplowed, and MI 107 is plowed only up to the ski area.

Camping: Porcupine Mountain Wilderness State Park and the Presque Isle River Unit.

Services: Restaurants and motels in Wakefield, nearby Ontonagon.

Nearby attractions: Ottawa National Forest, Lake Gogebic, Ontonagon Light in Ontonagon.

 The drive

You begin this drive to the Porcupine Mountain Wilderness from the town of Wakefield. Once in Wakefield, take CR 519 North. You immediately pass Indianhead Resort on your left. After 2 miles, you drive through a pastoral area called Connorville. During the next several miles, you begin to experience the deep undulations of the road as you rise and fall while surrounded by a thick needleleaf forest. Shortly after passing the Sand Island Creek, you ascend a steep hill. As you reach the hill's crest, you can see Lake Superior straight ahead.

About 14 miles from Wakefield, the road travels along the Presque Isle River, roiling away through the woods. You pass Iagoo Falls on your right.

You then come to the intersection of CR 519 and South Boundary Road. You are near one of two entrances to the Porcupine Mountain Wilderness area, the southwest entrance. Continue straight to the water's edge as you pass the Nawadaha Falls on your right and then Manido Falls, also to your right. These falls are named after Ojibwe Indian *manitous*, or "spirit warriors." At the end of the road is the Porcupine Mountains State Park

Drive 14: Wakefield to Porcupine Mountain Wilderness State Park

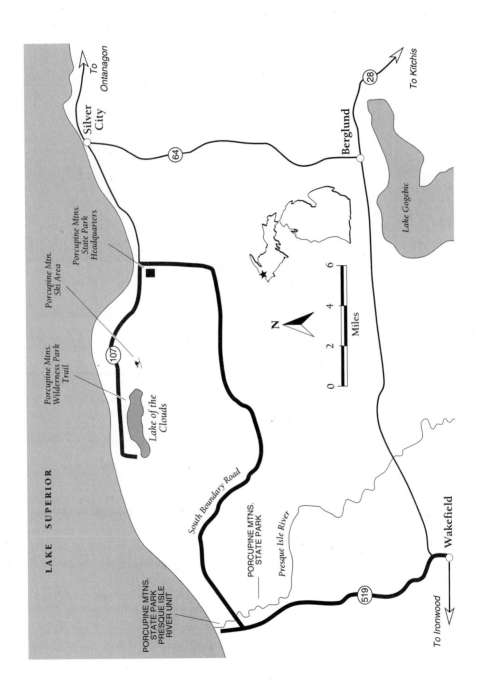

This sign marks the entrance to one of the nation's largest unspoiled natural areas.

Presque Isle River Unit. Manabezho Falls can be found toward the shore. There are campsites at this section of the Porcupines.

To drive to the other entrance, which is at the northeast side of the Porcupine Mountain Wilderness State Park, backtrack out of the parking lot to the intersection of CR 519 and South Boundary Road, and turn left. (South Boundary Road is plowed only through the end of November.) Follow South Boundary Road easterly for about 9 miles. There are deep, dense hills to your left and right. This road has plenty of curve to it. When you arrive at the Nonesuch Falls, which are to your right after you have driven about 9 miles, the road will turn due north and you will drive for about 6 miles to the intersection of South Boundary Road and MI 107. (MI 107 is plowed year-round only as far as the ski area.) At this intersection you will see signs for Porcupine Wilderness State Park. Turn left into the park. You will find the visitor center here. This is a good place to stop and find out more about the area. The park rangers are friendly and knowledgeable, and the center uses a variety of mediums to help you understand the history and geology of the park.

The Porcupine Mountain Wilderness State Park is an area of 60,000 pristine, remote acres, and is one of the few remaining unspoiled areas of our time. Towering pines and boreal forest trees huddle around nearby lakes, as if trying to hush them from the sounds of the world. There are miles of wild rivers in this park, and nooks and cranny's that may never have been seen by human eyes.

This area was once called *Kaugabissing*, which means "place of the porcupine" in Ojibwe. The ridges of the escarpment that cascade so ruggedly into the lake resemble the back of a porcupine. The Porcupine Wilderness, located in the Lake Superior snowbelt, receives an average snowfall of 175 inches per year. The area was established in 1945 as an act of the Michigan Legislature. Today the Department of Natural Resources maintains the more than 90 miles of foot trails threading through the area.

This area was not always a recreational spot for those who appreciate vast expanses of wild terrain. In 1841, the Porkies were rich in copper, and miners rushed here to unearth the valuable metal. Eventually loggers replaced the miners, but the rugged Porcupines proved too rugged a land for successful timbering.

You can camp at the state park, and there are also sixteen rustic cabins along some of the trails. Reservations are made years in advance, but the solitude and reverance that comes with them makes it well worth the wait.

For the grand finale of this drive, travel MI 107 west out of the parking lot for about 8 miles to the end of the road for a spectacular view of Lake of the Clouds. A pristine, natural lake that seems magically deposited into the heaviest, thickest portion of a forest, Lake of the Clouds is probably one of the most visited and photographed areas in Michigan.

Manido Falls on the Presque Isle River.

15

Sidnaw to Baraga

Sturgeon Gorge

General description: The 25-mile drive from Sidnaw to Baraga in the upper peninsula of Michigan escorts you to Sturgeon River Gorge Area. Exceptionally thick stands of pine and cedar trees encroach upon the road which rises and falls sharply. You eventually reach the highest point of the drive at Silver Mountain, then proceed north to Baraga, located on the shore of Lake Superior.

Special attractions: Sturgeon River Gorge Area, Ottawa National Forest, thick wet bogs and lush cedar and fir trees, Silver Mountain, rolling hills, Bear's Den Scenic Overlook.

Location: The northwest portion of the upper peninsula.

Drive route numbers: Michigan Highway 28, Forest Highway 2200, Forest Highway 2270, and Michigan Highway 38.

Travel season: Late spring, summer, and fall. Check with the Highway Department during questionable weather.

Camping: Baraga State Park.

Services: Limited services in Sidnaw. Baraga is filled with cafes, restaurants, and motels.

Nearby attractions: Shrine of the Snowshoe Priest, Hanka Homestead, Sylvania Wilderness Tract, Canyon Falls and Gorge just south of L'Anse, and the Calumet Opera House in Calumet.

 ## The drive

Start this drive in Sidnaw, a small town with a few services. You can reach Sidnaw by taking MI 28 in from the west or the east. In Sidnaw, turn north on Forest Highway 2200 which is also known as Pequet Lake Road. This well-maintained gravel road winds through scenic low-lying wetland and bog terrain. The bogs are surrounded by some edge forests containing a mix of old birch, pine, and hardwood trees. Eventually, this edge forest yields to a stand of white pine trees. This portion of the drive is located in the heart of the Ottawa National Forest, a 928,000-acre forest characterized by rocky outcroppings of basalt. It is hilly, curvy, and beautiful.

A few miles out of Sidnaw you will come to a one-lane bridge spanning the Sturgeon River. The Sturgeon River is 25 miles long and lined with

Drive 15: Sidnaw to Baraga
Sturgeon Gorge

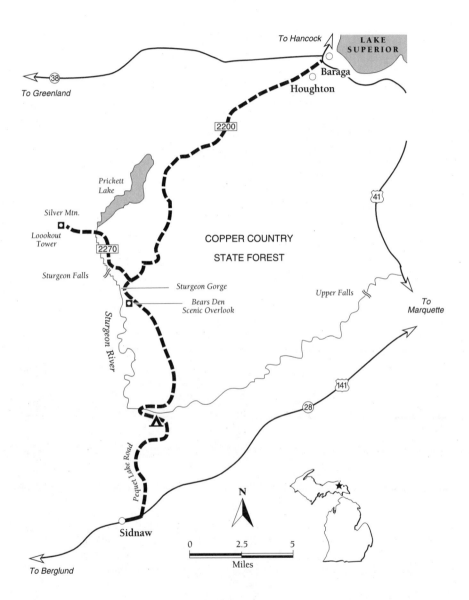

To Hancock

LAKE SUPERIOR

To Greenland
38

Baraga
Houghton

2200

Prickett Lake

Silver Mtn.

Loookout Tower

2270

COPPER COUNTRY

STATE FOREST

41

Sturgeon Falls

Sturgeon Gorge

Bears Den Scenic Overlook

Upper Falls

To Marquette

Sturgeon River

141

28

Pequet Lake Road

N

Sidnaw

To Berglund

0   2.5   5

Miles

natural virgin balsam fir and other dense needleleaf trees as well as mixed hardwood trees. This makes a preferred habitat for eagles and otters. To the left is the Sturgeon Road Campground.

In a few miles the road will come to a Y at the intersection of Forest Highways 2200 and 2236. At this point continue on Forest Highway 2200. The slow gentle curves of the road are lined with huge white birch and poplar trees. The forest floor is brimming with bracken fern and thick wooly mosses.

You can only travel this road late spring, summer, and fall. In winter this is a snowmobile trail offering exceptional beauty when the fir and cedar trees are covered with fresh dustings of snow.

Leaving this area, you begin to travel through hardwood forest again. The hillside view unveils a mixture of pine and birch trees, and the road takes on challenging turns as you crest the top of the hill. One mile later the road begins to straighten. To your right, you will notice a large open space— an area that appears to have been recently clear cut. One mile later you drop back into a canopy-covered road as you travel through a dense forest. Just before you reach Sturgeon Gorge, you will come to Bears Den Scenic Overlook which holds a sweeping view of the gorge.

As you reach the gorge area there will be signs directing you left into the parking area. It is a long, rugged switchback walk to the bottom of the

Pathway down to Sturgeon River Gorge.

gorge, which is some 400 feet deep. The natural relationship between water and rock is phenomenal. Watching as the gorge walls are being pounded, pushed, and beaten by the water, it is easy to understand how water can create formations of mammoth proportions. The forest area surrounding the gorge is thick with cedar trees dripping with moisture and aroma. Moss, fern, and lichens grow thick here.

Leaving the gorge area, you will come to another Y in the road. Forest Highway 2200 heads northeast, to your right; and Forest Highway 2270, to your left, goes north to Silver Mountain. Follow the Y to the left, staying on Forest Highway 2270. Here, the gorge's waterfall is to your left. You have to look carefully to find the access point, but it is well worth the trip. Continuing north, you will twist and crest your way to the highest point of this drive. This area, called Silver Mountain, was carved by glaciers, leaving a dome-shaped creation. The 1,312-foot peak was once the site of a fire tower. Enter the parking lot on your left. To reach the summit, take a long, steep stairway leading to the top of Silver Mountain. Although it is a long and somewhat difficult climb, the view of the Sturgeon River Gorge Wilderness area is many miles deep and very rewarding.

Back in your car, drive back to Forest Road 2200 and continue north toward Baraga. This portion of the road begins your descent through thick forest. Continue for several miles until you reach MI 38. Turn right. From here it is only about 12 miles into the town of Baraga, which is located on the shore of Lake Superior's L'Anse Bay.

Once you are in Baraga, you can turn right on US 141 and finish this drive at the entrance to Baraga State Park. The Park is situated on the shore of Lake Superior and offers swimming, boating, and more than one hundred campsites. This is typically a busy campground due to the wonderful location for boaters.

16

Norway to Wakefield

Piers Gorge

General description: This 131-mile drive from Norway to Wakefield takes you through Piers Gorge, a wide rushing portion of the Menominee River, which creates the boundary between Michigan and Wisconsin. You will pass through lush, thick needleleaf forest while crossing small creeks and streams, proceeding through iron mine territory, and the Sylvania Wilderness Recreational Area.

Special attractions: Piers Gorge, Menominee River, Sand Portage Falls, Niagara Dam, Iron Mountain Iron Mine, Cornish Pump and Mining Museum, Twin Falls Dam, Spread Eagle Chain of Lakes, Bewabic State Park, Sylvania Wilderness Recreation Area, Lake Gogebic.

Location: Begins in the southwest portion of the upper peninsula and proceeds northwest into the interior of it.

Drive route numbers: U.S. Highway 2, Piers Gorge Road, U.S. Highway 8, U.S. Highway 141, Thousand Island Road, Michigan Highway 64.

Travel season: Year-round.

Camping: Bewabic State Park, Sylvania Wilderness Area, Lake Gogebic.

Services: Food and lodging in Norway, Wakefield, Iron Mountain, Iron River.

Nearby attractions: Porcupine Mountains Wilderness Area, Escanaba, Menominee, J. W. Wells State Park.

The drive

You will experience the rushing power of water as it moves within rocky shores and cedar lined banks. This drive takes you from Norway to Wakefield through a place called Piers Gorge, which is a wide and beautiful spot in the Menominee River. The Menominee River, located in the western upper peninsula, forms the boundary between Wisconsin and Michigan.

You will find the starting point for this drive in Norway on US 8. You can reach Norway by taking US 2 from the east or the west. Begin this drive by turning south on US 8 in the heart of Norway. Follow it for 2 miles to Piers Gorge Road. Turn right. This road to Piers Gorge is not plowed in winter, so this portion is a spring, summer, and fall drive only.

When you reach the parking area of Piers Gorge, there will be a level

Drive 16: Norway to Wakefield
Piers Gorge

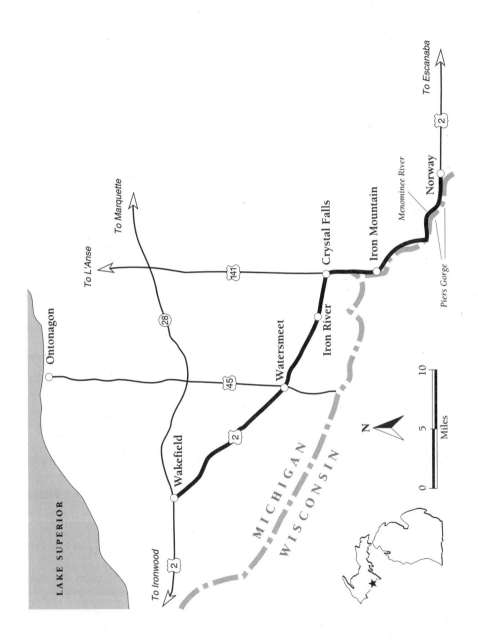

walking path which plods through a wetland emitting the aroma of moist cedar. The entire walk isn't very far; round trip it's about 1.5 miles. From this point you can see the different stones in the river's mighty banks, as well as the cuts and crevices that have been carved out by years of moving water. The gorge is cut into steep walls of bedrock that loom some 70 feet high. Water rushes over the walls and creates four distinct waterfalls, each unique in size, velocity, and mystique.

As you leave the parking area and head back out on US 8 proceeding south, you will come to another waterfall to your right after about 3 miles. This is Sand Portage Falls. Continue on for 2 more miles to reach Niagara Dam, which is to your right. A beautiful hill of hardwood trees will be to your left.

Once you have passed Niagara Dam, you will come to the intersection of US 8 and US 141. Turn right onto US 141. From here you will proceed north. Driving north you will immediately cross the Menominee River. To your left and right are views of the river as it twirls and rolls underneath the road.

The Menominee River creates a serviceable habitat for bald eagles, who like to roost in the tall trees near water so they can fish in the shallows. The bald eagle, or *Haliaeetus leucocephalos*, is our national bird. It has been making a steady comeback since its near extinction in the 1960s.

Still traveling north on US 141 (about 2.5 miles from Niagara Dam), you will see US 2 come in from your right. Proceed past this merge and continue northwest toward Iron Mountain. At this point US 141 is also referred to as US 2 and MI 95.

You will reach Iron Mountain after about 3 more miles. This town is the heart of the Menominee Range, one of three upper peninsula iron-ore belts. It was the allure of white pine for timber that first attracted settlers in the mid-1800s. When the trees were logged and the forests bare, mining replaced lumbering as the area's livelihood. To learn more about the mining industry, you can take a side trip to the Iron Mountain Iron Mine, which can be explored by taking US 2 east for 10 miles to Vulcan. At this mine you can explore 2,600 feet of underground tunnels and view large, hollow caverns. The first tunnel was dug in 1870 when the mines had the ability to attract immigrants as laborers. The mine closed in 1945 when the availability of power shovels made open pit mining an economically advantageous operation.

You can also stop at the Cornish Pump and Mining Museum, located in the heart of Iron Mountain—home to a 725-ton water pump, the nation's largest in 1890. This was used to pump water from the Chapin Iron Mine, the largest producing mine on the Menominee Range. Pumping two hundred tons of water per minute, this piece of machinery needed over eleven

Marshy areas appear prairie-like from Norway to Wakefiled.

thousand tons of coal per year to operate.

Leave Iron Mountain by proceeding north on US 2, also called MI 95 and US 141 at this point. Almost immediately, you will pass Lake Antoine, on your right. This lake has a lovely wooded picnic area and beach.

Shortly after the picnic area and beach, the road will come to a Y. Follow US 141 to the left as MI 95 veers to the right. You will pass Twin Falls Dam to your right and immediately cross the Menominee River once more, this time ending just south of it, which means you are in Wisconsin for this short portion of the drive.

Approximately 6 miles past that point you begin to weave through the Spread Eagle Chain of Lakes which are situated to your right. There are plenty of other small, shallow lakes situated to your left. Continue making your way north for about 20 miles until you arrive in Crystal Falls. In the middle of town you will turn left on US 141/US 2. One half mile out of town the road separates and US 141 will proceed directly north. Stay on US 2 traveling northwest.

You will reach Bewabic State Park just 3 miles out of town. This state park is situated to your left on Second Lake and First Lake. Driving west past Bewabic State Park, you will begin to enter a portion of the drive that dips into valleys of hardwood trees, and rebounds into wetland areas. The landscape will start to gently rise and fall in peaks and valleys, with mixed lowland forest creating soft, full edges around the moist land. This continues to varying degrees for the next 12 miles until you reach Iron River.

Iron River has a population of approximately 2,500. Named after the Iron River, this town boasts a terrific museum called the Iron County Historical Museum. It is an 8-acre complex that depicts loggers, pioneers, and miners in exhibits distributed in 20 buildings. At this site is the oldest steel headframe in the midwest, which is over 108 feet tall and on the National Register of Historic Places.

Leaving Iron River and heading toward Wakefield, you will enter a portion of the road blessed with deep undulations of combination forest stalwarts such as maple and birch trees.

About 13 miles out of Iron River you will pass Golden Lake, to your right. The road levels out as you continue through a magnificent forest. About 6 miles past Golden Lake you will cross the intersection of US 2 and Forest Highway 3920. Here, you will enter a low spruce swamp and then slowly elevate out of the marsh area. You will then see Imp Lake located on your left.

About 6 miles later, as you pass through Watersmeet, you will be in the vicinity of the Sylvania Wilderness and Recreational Area, a 21,000-acre area of unspoiled environment. It offers the Clark Day Use Area, an 820-acre lake with a sandy beach, surrounded by the edges of hardwood forest. There is an 8-mile hiking trail which takes you around Clark Lake where you may see exceptional wildlife such as barred owls, pileated woodpeckers, warblers, and fishers (members of the weasel family). In addition, the area boasts the Sylvania Canoe System, which has more than 4,000 acres of water and 25 miles of portages. This system connects 29 lakes and may be traveled by non-motorized craft only.

To reach the Sylvania Wilderness and Recreation Area from Watersmeet, travel west on US 2 for about 2 miles. Turn left on Thousand Island Road and proceed south for 4 miles to the recreation area.

Return to US 2 and proceed for 23 miles through mixed forest and wetland. At 24 miles past Sylvania, you will pass, on your right, the access to Lake Gogebic. To reach the lake, turn right on MI 64 and head north for 4 miles. Gogebic, the largest lake in the interior of the upper peninsula, is 13, 380 acres and known for good fishing and snowfalls that average over 200 inches per year.

Wakefield, the end of this drive, is about 16 miles past Lake Gogebic. This small town was named for George M. Wakefield, who was the town site surveyor and person responsible for platting the town.

17

Manistique to St. Ignace

General description: This drive travels a portion of the southern border of Michigan's upper peninsula. From Manistique to St. Ignace, you will experience 88 miles of various Lake Michigan shoreline and hardwood forest. The drive continues away from the shore for about 27 miles between Gulliver and Naubinway, but finishes up again along the sandy shore all the way from Naubinway to St. Ignace. Many roadside picnic areas and scenic turnouts allow breathtaking views of Lake Michigan and its various shoreline features.

Special attractions: Sweeping shoreline views, sandy beaches, scenic outlooks, Father Marquette Historical Marker, Epoufette.

Location: The lower southeastern edge of the upper peninsula.

Drive route numbers: U.S. Highway 2 East.

Travel Season: Year-round. Summer is busiest time for walkers and hikers. Heavy snows can close roads in winter.

Camping: Indian Lake State Park, Palms Brook State Park in Manistique, Straits State Park in St. Ignace.

Services: Hotels, motels, resorts, cafes, gift shops, and gas stations dot the entire journey.

Nearby attractions: Fort De Baude in St. Ignace, Hog Island Point State Forest, Mackinac Island, Mackinaw City.

 ## The drive

Begin the drive by picking up US 2 East in the quaint fishing town of Manistique. (If you are coming from the northern portion of the upper peninsula, you can reach US 2 East by taking Michigan Highway 94 south.)

With a population of 4,800, Manistique boasts a real working pier with a fish market, plenty of fishing and recreation boats, docks, and seagulls. The beautiful waters of the Manistique River served as impetus for this town's name. Founded by Henry Rowe Schoolcraft, Indian agent for the Ojibwe, the town was originally called *Monistique*, after the Ojibwe word for the vermilion color of the river's water. A spelling error on the land title permanently altered the name to Manistique.

US 2 East begins in the heart of Manistique. As you edge out of town approximately 1.5 miles, the Lake Michigan shoreline suddenly appears.

Drive 17: Manistique to St. Ignace

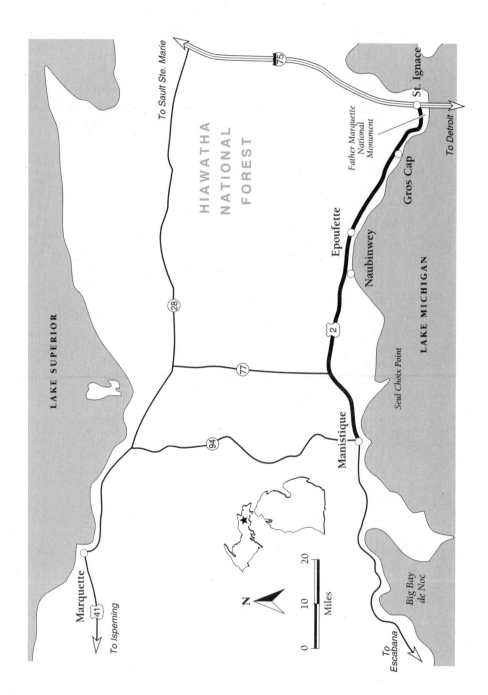

CLIMB IT
HIKE IT
FLOAT IT
BIKE IT

A FALCON GUIDE

Whatever you do outside, helps you find a better place to do it. Maps, photos, safety tips, and charts accompany detailed descriptions of state-by-state rock climbing sites, hiking trails, river routes, and mountain biking trails. Falcon also publishes information about many more outdoor activities and nature gift ideas.

For a free catalog of books, maps, recreational guidebooks, and nature gift ideas, please return this card with the following information.

Name _____

Address _____

City _____

State _____ Zip _____

❏ **YES!** I'd like to send a catalog to a friend.

Name _____

Address _____

City _____

State _____ Zip _____

Or call for a **FREE** catalog.

1-800-582-2665

FALCON®
P.O. BOX 1718
HELENA,
MONTANA
59624

NO POSTAGE
NECESSARY
IF MAILED
IN THE
UNITED STATES

FALCON™

BUSINESS REPLY MAIL
FIRST-CLASS MAIL PERMIT NO 80 HELENA MT

POSTAGE WILL BE PAID BY ADDRESSEE

FALCON PRESS PUBLISHING CO
PO BOX 1718
HELENA MT 59624-9948

Grand Sable Dunes, Grand Marais, Michigan (Drive 8).

Top: *Grand Traverse Light (Drive 23).*
Bottom: *Carp River Inlet, PMWSP (Drive 14).*

Top: *Marquette Lighthouse (Drive 17)*.
Bottom: *Blue Heron, Seney National Refuge (Drive 9)*.

Top: *Big Bay (B&B) lighthouse, Northern Michigan (Drive 10).*
Bottom: *Aerial View, Copper Harbor Light (Drive 11).*

Top: *Point Iroquois Light (Drive 6).*
Bottom: *Whitefish Point (Drive 6).*

Top: *Miner's Castle and Falls (Drive 8).*
Bottom: *Seney Wildlife Refuge (Drive 9).*

Top: *Porcupine Mountain State Park, Manido Falls (Drive 14).*
Bottom: *Munising Falls (Drive 8).*

White Pine, Black River Harbor (Drive 13).

Signs for the Manistique Town Beach signal you to turn right into the beach parking area. Here, soft velvety beaches are open to walkers, hikers, swimmers, and vista seekers. The area has one of the nicest boardwalk systems in the upper peninsula. Sturdy wooden structures parallel the beach and allow visitors to walk with ease amid the deep, wind-tossed sand. Enjoy the view of the Manistique East Breakwater Lighthouse, an outstanding red salute to the tough waters breaking on the sandy shore here. Stop and join the boardwalk at one of the two or three beach access points out of Manistique, which are placed about 1 mile apart.

Continuing east on US 2, you will find the road generally hugging the shoreline for the next 9 miles. Passengers can catch glimpses of Lake Michigan on the right (south), through dense stands of white pine trees.

This drive is also part of the Lake Michigan Circle Tour Drive, a drive that takes you along the entire shore of Lake Michigan. The complete length of the Circle Tour Drive is approximately 1,100 shoreline miles. The Circle Tour miles are well marked with Circle Tour Route signs at every 10-mile interval. For more information on the Circle Tour Drive of Lake Michigan, call the Michigan Travel Bureau at 1-800-5432-YES, extension 344.

Approximately 14 miles out of Manistique is the town of Gulliver. Gulliver Lake will appear to your right (south) and interrupt the view of Lake Michigan. The road departs here from the shore to creep northward for 11 miles. Rolling pastures, meadows plump with wildflowers, and bogs dotted with waterfowl are the scenic backdrop along this portion of the drive. A roadside park, a good place to stop and stretch, is available along this section. Two miles farther down this road, you will come to the intersection of MI 77 and US 2 East.

For a side trip to the Seney National Wildlife Refuge, turn left onto MI 77 and head northward for 18 miles. The refuge is 3 miles north of Germfask. The Seney refuge boasts more than 200 species of birds including bald eagle, sandhill crane, and various other waterfowl. Other wildlife reside here too, such as black bears, deer, beavers, and otters. This 25,000-acre area features the Strangmoor Bog, a natural national landmark. The Strangmoor Bog is actually several small "string-like" bogs which alternate with sand dunes. Hiking is the only means to reach the Bog, and you must obtain permission to do so. These bogs are typically found in arctic or subarctic regions, so do not miss the chance to view them here. (Seney National Wildlife Refuge is detailed in Drive 24 in this guide.)

From the intersection of US 2 and MI 77, the road soon darts toward the east and then continues on a straight line through Lake Superior State Forest. Follow the road for the next few miles through a true northern hardwood tree community (typical and widespread in this area). This portion of the drive is characterized by a tapestry of many ecosystems, including pine forest, conifer bog, and deciduous swamp.

There are plenty of amenities along this entire drive. Small motels come in every shape, size, color, and notion. There are literally dozens of campgrounds with or without cabins, as well as charming cafes and small-town gas stations. You are never more than a stone's throw from food, rest, or shelter. Although the myriad of amenities disrupts the natural environment, the availability of services adds a recreational charm to the area.

Eastern white pine trees, characterized by dark gray, deeply etched bark and long, slender needles, flourish throughout this drive, as well as in most parts of the upper peninsula. Sugar maple, beech, and yellow birch trees also grow well here. Of all conebearing trees, the pines loom largest. There are approximately thirty-six species of pine growing in the United States, three of which are native to Michigan. The upper peninsula forest of years past was dominated by white and red pine trees. Some hardwood trees mingled, but it was truly the pine forest that gave this land its life and commerce. As Michigan's state tree, white pine was the major tree harvested during the peak of the lumber industry so predominant in Michigan history. The red pine you will notice on this portion of the drive stands approximately the same height as the white pine. Red pine thrives in acidic sandy soil and rocky outcrops like the rocky terrain near the shoreline.

Reaching Naubinway, 46 miles into the drive, the road returns to the

Entrance to Seul Choix Point Lighthouse.

shoreline. This begins the most outstanding section of the drive, where the road gently nuzzles the coast until the port of St. Ignace. About 3 miles out of Naubinway, you begin driving a portion of the road where US 2 is also known as Lake Michigan Scenic Highway, a brief part of the Lake Michigan Circle Tour. Notice the aqua blue color of the water at this point. The shoreline view to the right (south) is offset by a natural boundry of white pine trees. In some spots, the fullness of the trees interrupts the view of the shore, but creates a picture no less stunning.

Halfway between Naubinway and journey's end is a small town called Epoufette, pronounced *eh'-poo-fer*. Some say that Epoufette was the first place that Father Marquette stopped on his journey from St. Ignace, where he and Louis Jolliet began their journey to map the Mississippi River. *Epoufette* is French for "place of rest." To explore Epoufette Bay, turn right onto Epoufette Road and follow it along the bay to its climax at Point Epoufette.

Continue on US 2 East along a more prominent windswept shore for the next 20 miles toward St. Ignace. Lazy, loping hills and mounds of soft-serve sand tumble into the water on the right (south), while the area to the left (north) is marsh-like and low. Watch for Canada geese, wood ducks, and seagulls on either side of the highway. Also look out for whitetail deer and moose. With a total population of more than one million in Michigan alone, whitetail deer are abundant in this area. Quick-moving and nervous, these animals, darting from shore to woods and back again, can surprise even the most careful driver. Moose are less common, but with a recently established moose herd that roams the upper peninsula, there is a chance that moose may be wandering the area, especially in the swamplike terrain.

As the shore begins to offer longer, deeper expanses of sand with wisps of tall green grasses, the amount of activity increases. People of all ages walk, hike, or jog leisurely along. About 7 miles before you reach St. Ignace, the road elevates for a good view of the lake as well as the rooftops of homes and resorts. Silouhetted in the foreground is the Mackinac Bridge, "Mighty Mac," a 5-mile suspension bridge which joins the upper and lower portions of Michigan, and crosses over the boundary between Lake Michigan and Lake Huron.

St. Ignace rises in the distance. This town was founded in 1671, when Jesuit missionary Father Jacques Marquette and a group of Huron Indians were fleeing a rival tribe. They built a mission and named it Saint Ignatius of Loyola, crediting it to the saint who was the founder of the Jesuit order. St. Ignace holds more than tourist fare and frolic. There is a national memorial, a museum and state park, all created in honor of Father Jacques Marquette. The exhibits and films here describe his life and highlight his accomplishments. Fort De Baude Museum, holding many collections featuring Indian and regional artifacts, including a dugout canoe and antique guns, is lo-

The kitchen area of Seul Choix Point Lighthouse.

cated on the site of an actual French fort, dating back to 1681.

Nearing the center of St. Ignace, turn north on I-75, then right onto Business I-75. It will take you through the downtown area of St. Ignace where bustling steetside shops, fudge makers, souvenir sellers, hotels, motels, and plenty of good food await the traveler. In the middle of town, you will find a harbor for recreational boats of every conceivable size, kind, and color. Most noticeable are the large ferry boats taking passengers across the Straits of Mackinac for a trip to Mackinac Island. St. Ignace is a hotspot for vacationers who intend to visit Mackinac Island.

Business I-75 follows the curve of the shoreline. St. Ignace is situated on the shore of the Straits of Mackinac, which you will see to your right. There are shops and motels to the left and right. As you drive through St. Ignace, the Star Line Mackinac Island Ferry is located to your right, on the shore. You can proceed north to the edge of town where you will find more hotels, restaurants, and shopping, or you can turn south and go back to I-75. From there, you can follow I-75 onto the Mackinac Bridge, over the Straits of Mackinac to the lower peninsula, detailed in Drive 5.

18

Mackinaw City to Sturgeon Bay

General description: This 10-mile drive from Mackinaw City to Sturgeon Bay takes you through Wilderness State Park along the lower peninsula's northern coast. The drive ends at Waugoshance Point, and during the brief miles you will find a variety of wildlife and captivating (if not scientifically interesting) wildflowers, such as the calypso orchid and the showy lady's slipper.

Special attractions: Waugoshance Point, Cecil's Bay, the beautiful flowers and curious wildlife.

Location: The extreme northwest portion of the lower peninsula.

Drive route numbers: Interstate 75, U.S. Highway 31, Central Avenue, Trails End Road, and County Road 81.

Travel Season: Year-round.

Camping: There are many private campgrounds and lakeside cabins in Mackinaw City.

Services: Terrific restaurants and shopping in Mackinaw City. A strip of hotels and shops line the water's edge in the middle of town.

Nearby attractions: Colonial Michilimackinac, Mackinaw Maritime Park in Macinaw City. McGulpin Point Light and Bois Blanc Island.

 The drive

You can reach Mackinaw City from the east from US 23 north, and from the south by way of I-75. On I-75 northbound into town, exit left on Central Avenue. In approximately 0.5 mile, Central Avenue will make a sharp left. In another 0.5 mile it will intersect with Trails End Road. Turn right at this intersection so you are traveling on Trails End Road. Take an immediate left onto CR 81, also known as Wilderness Park Drive. (See Drive 5 for information on Mackinaw City.)

Wilderness State Park is open year-round and has 250 campsites spread over 2 campgrounds. Situated on Lake Michigan, it offers picnic areas, modern toilets, and showers, as well as rustic cabins. The park includes more than 8,000 acres, which qualifies it as one of the lower peninsula's largest state parks. Also one of the least developed parks in the state, this area is a pristine and inspiring place for watchers of wildlife and wildflowers.

Drive 18: Mackinaw City to Sturgeon Bay

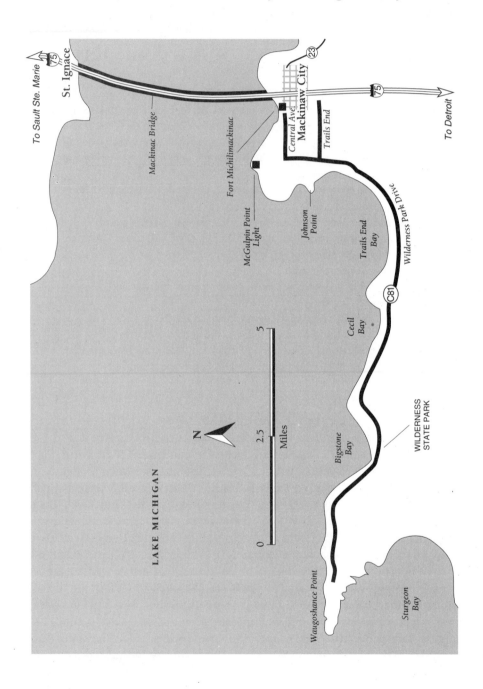

As you begin this portion of the drive, you immediately round the soft edge of Lake Michigan's Trails End Bay, which is to your right. After about 3 miles you are farther away from the lake due to a simple curve of land that dips into the lake and divides Trails End Bay from Cecil Bay. You pass Cecil Bay on your right after 1 more mile.

Farther on and again to your right, you pass Big Stone Bay, a small cozy nook of water. Canada Goose Pond is to your left. Both the bay and the pond are good spots to watch waterfowl.

As you follow Wilderness Park Drive to the west for another 6 miles, you will reach its end. Situated at the end of the road is Waugoshance Point, with a shore that juts out into Lake Michigan, and a view of Sturgeon Bay. It also offers a view of four lighthouses standing out in the depths of the lake. The lighthouse farthest to the north, on your far right, is White Shoal Light. The one closest to land is Waugoshance Light. Next to it, continuing to your left, is Grays Reef Light. Finally, to your far left is the southernmost light, Skilligallee Light. Some are still working, and some are not. At the end of the point you can also see two islands, Temperance Island and Waugoshance Island, both part of Wilderness State Park. The purpose of the lighthouses is to guide boaters and freighter pilots between the islands.

Waugoshance Point is an excellent spot for birders. Home to more than one hundred species of birds, this is a popular nesting area, migration route, and rest stop for many of those species. The point is closed during the nesting season of the Great Lakes piping plover, a rare Michigan bird.

At the east edge of the park you will find thick stands of virgin hemlock and Norway pine trees looming more than 100 feet overhead. These trees make good habitat for owls and pileated woodpeckers. The large abandoned cavities of these trees make wonderful nesting areas. The pileated woodpecker is approximately the size of a crow, and is characterized by a black and white body and a red splash of color on top of its head.

One of the gems of this park is the variety of wildflowers. Park headquarters is a good place to ask the location of the latest and best blooms. Wild orchid and rose pogonia grow well here due to the soft, wet ground. The rose pogonia can reach heights of 2 feet and has delicate pinkish-to-white flowers on top of an erect stem. This kind of flower favors wet meadows and swamp terrain. The calypso orchid also favors cool, moist conditions. *Calypso bulbosa* is a small and delightful orchid that reaches a height of only 2 to 8 inches. Its rose-colored flower blushes around a yellow middle.

Probably one of the most interesting and sought after flowers is the showy lady's slipper, which is abundant in this area. *Cyprpedium reginae* makes its home in moist woods and wetlands. This flower, Minnesota's state flower, is also the provincial emblem of Prince Edward Island. This flower grows up to 3 feet tall. A key identifier for this flower is its trademark pouch-

Wilderness State Park is filled with wildflowers in the spring and summer months.

like lower petal. The lady slipper depends on the pollination process to multiply. But it is no easy feat. The pouch contains no nectar, but gives off a phantom nectar-like scent which woos bees. Bees smell this ghostly scent, descend the channel into the pouch, and with no nectar to feed on and only one escape route, the bees squeeze through one of two egress channels. As they do, their backs gets pollinated. Repeating the process in the next lady slipper pollinates the next flower.

After exploring the park and its natural wonders, you can take Wilderness Park Drive eastward back to Mackinaw City. To travel a different route back, follow Wilderness Park Drive east as far as the intersection of CR 81. Turn right and travel south into Mackinaw State Forest. After 5 miles, you can turn left onto Gill Road, and in 4 more miles turn left (north) onto US 31 which takes you back up to Mackinaw City.

19

Harbor Springs to Cross Village
Tunnel of Trees

General description: One of Michigan's most spectacular drives, Michigan Highway 119 leaves the exclusive resort town of Harbor Springs, whisks you through an area once largely inhabited by the Odawa, or Ottawa Indians, and ventures north 20 miles to the town of Cross Village. This narrow road becomes engulfed in the overstory of a mixed forest, dominated by mature broadleaf and pine trees. Known as the "tunnel of trees," the scenic beauty of this drive is splendid in the spring or summer, but offers special majesty during peak autumn color.

Special attractions: The biggest attraction is the canopy of trees that surrounds you as you drive along the shore of Lake Michigan.

Location: The northwest portion of the lower peninsula.

Drive route numbers: Michigan Highway 119.

Travel season: Year-round. The road is spectacular; crowded in autumn.

Camping: None on the drive, but camping is available in Wilderness State Park in Sturgeon Bay, north of Cross Village.

Services: Quaint cafes and baked goods are the best bet in Harbor Springs, along with a few good restaurants. There are limited services along the length of the drive.

Nearby attractions: Wilderness State Park in Sturgeon Bay, Mackinaw City.

 The drive

Begin this drive in the wealthy resort town of Harbor Springs, located in the northwestern portion of the lower peninsula on the shore of Lake Michigan's Little Traverse Bay. Harbor Springs was once a logging town, as were many northern Michigan towns. When the lumber industry went bust in the late 1800s, the railroad, which was located in nearby Petoskey, needed an alternative to the lumber they had been hauling. They marketed the area as a recreational hotspot and as a refuge for hay fever sufferers. The railroad then began carting resorters (most from the wealthiest families of Detroit, Chicago, and St. Louis) to the area.

Downtown Harbor Springs makes you feel you are stepping back into the early 1900s. Main street is filled with Victorian storefronts and quaint

Drive 19: Harbor Springs to Cross Village
Tunnel of Trees

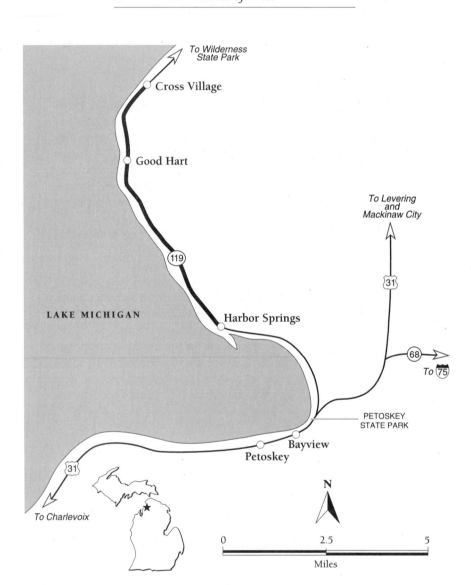

To Wilderness
State Park

Cross Village

Good Hart

To Levering
and
Mackinaw City

119

31

LAKE MICHIGAN

Harbor Springs

68

To 75

PETOSKEY
STATE PARK

Bayview
Petoskey

31

To Charlevoix

N

0   2.5   5

Miles

cottage shops. You will find galleries, cozy bakeries, coffee shops, and unique gift shops. For a bird's-eye view of the town's downtown area, as well as of the boat-filled harbor, take a short side trip called the East Bluff Drive. Take MI 119 east past the State Street intersection. Proceed to the end of the road. Park here and take the stairway to a scenic overlook. In July and August, the harbor is especially busy—a good time to spot colorful watercraft of all types.

You can also drive through the Victorian downtown by following Main Street between State and Gardner, in the heart of Harbor Springs. Here you will find remnants of days gone by, including the Andrew Blackbird Museum. Andrew Blackbird, an Odawa Chief, established the first post office in Harbor Springs in 1862. The post office was in Blackbird's kitchen. Eventually, Blackbird built another room next to his home so he could handle the increase in mail. As the area became settled by whites, many resident Indians, like Chief Blackbird, lost the paid government positions they held. His home stands on Main Street as a reminder of the area's colorful past. It is filled with artifacts from Blackbird's life such as Odawa birch bark baskets, Indian clothing, and more.

Next door to the Andrew Blackbird Museum is an odd-looking, hexagonal house called the Shay House. This winged structure was built in 1892 by Ephraim Shay, inventor of a small, quick locomotive that would eventually revolutionize the industry. Built in 1881, the locomotive was slim and small, allowing access to remote places, like the deep forests of Michigan.

Harbor Springs also has an exclusive century-old colony of homes called Wequetonsing (pronounced *WEE-kwee-Ton-sing,* or *WEE-kwee* for short). Now an organized residential association with strict regulations governing grounds, structure, and style of repairs and additions, it is a beautiful area. To reach it, follow Bay Street east to Zoll, turn south to the shore, and then left onto Beach Drive. This neighborhood is brimming with architecture from the late 1800s. Sprawling porches, colorful flower beds, cookie cutter windows, and gingerbread trim adorn these homes which were established by Presbyterians from Allegan, Michigan and Elkhart, Indiana. This association was modeled after the successful association in Petoskey, called Bay View. You can learn more about Bay View in Drive 20.

The area between Harbor Springs and Cross Village, once called L'Arbre Croche, was inhabited by Odawa, or Ottawa Indians, in the 1700s. While many Indians from the southern portion of the lower peninsula were forced west by the United States Government, the Ottawa people were able to retain their villages because wealthy resorters bought many of their crafts and quillwork. Today, the Ottawa population has diminished greatly, with the largest concentrations remaining near the area of Cross Village.

Begin this drive by taking MI 119 north toward Cross Village. MI 119

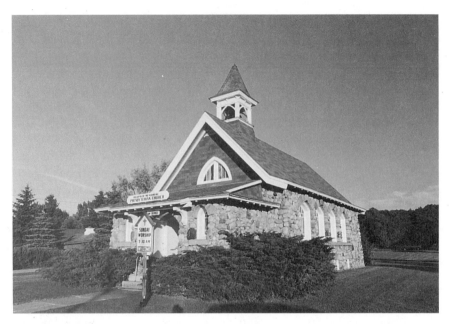

The Ridpath Memorial Presbyterian Church in Cross Village.

is a narrow two-lane road that pitches, sways, and swoops through thick hardwood and pine trees growing along the shore of Lake Michigan.

As you leave Harbor Springs on MI 119, the road gently elevates you above the tops of the trees—splendid views abound. To your left (west), depending on how dense the foliage is, you can see splashes of blue from Lake Michigan waters.

One mile out of Harbor Springs, you will pass through West Traverse Village. Here, the road will become quite narrow, hilly, and winding. This kind of road continues for the next 20 miles. This drive can be very busy during the summer and fall months. Be prepared to take your time. There are not many opportunities to pass, so relax and use every moment to peek into the thick, enchanting forest.

After 7 miles, overstory begins to engulf the road—you will realize why the drive is called the "Tunnel of Trees." In autumn especially, the foliage from trees on either side of the road meets high over the middle of the road where it forms a canopy so soft that it lets daylight trickle through in small amounts only. The deciduous trees in this canopy are primarily beech, maple, and birch. This is a mixed forest, in which young broadleaf trees mingle with mature species, such as red oak. There are areas of white pine and fir trees here as well.

Fourteen miles out of Harbor Springs, the forest floor is covered with large white flowers known as trilliums, a lovely, hardy member of the lily family. Thriving best in moist woods, such as this area near Lake Michigan, the trillium boasts three broad leaves and three showy petals. Other names for the trillum are white wood lily or wake-robin. This handsome flower turns pink as it ages and typically blooms in May. You can see the trillium on any portion of this drive, but the area here seems to have an abundance of them.

After 19 miles, you come to Cross Village. Established by French missionaries in the 1700s, this area was once one of the largest Indian missions in the United States. Cross Village is so small you hardly notice you are in a town. It does have one restaurant that plays an important historical role. The main building you see in town is an old, weathered-looking eatery called Legs Inn. The inn was originally built by a Polish immigrant named Stanley Smolak. Smolak came to the United States to work in an auto factory. Around the decade of the 1920s, he became friends with the Ottawa Indians of Cross Village, and was inducted into their tribe. They called him "Chief White Cloud." Smolak then went to work building the inn which he filled to the brim with hand-carved pieces of driftwood. Smolak served his favorite homeland dishes, and soon his restaurant became something of a landmark. The restaurant still specializes in Polish meals, and the interesting driftwood carvings and furniture remain. In addition to the Legs Inn, you can find gas and convenience items in town.

You can either travel back to Harbor Springs, or continue north on MI 119 toward Mackinaw State Forest. MI 119 north out of Cross Village turns into Lake Shore Drive. Follow it north along the shore, and after 5 miles you will pass Township Park on your left. Continue north and in 2 miles the road darts to the right and becomes Lakeview Road. Proceed east for approximately 10 miles until it meets US 31. From there, you can proceed north to Mackinaw City. See Drive 5 for more information on Mackinaw City.

20

Charlevoix to Harbor Springs
Petoskey and Bay View

General description: This 25-mile drive begins in the busy resort town of Charlevoix, passes the location that was once the only kingdom that ever existed on United States soil, also passes an elite summer colony on the shore of Lake Michigan, and arrives in the lovely town of Harbor Springs.
Special attractions: Beaver Island, Bay View, Petoskey State Park.
Location: The northwest portion of the lower peninsula.
Drive route numbers: U.S. Highway 31, Michigan Highway 22, Michigan Highway 119
Travel season: Year-round.
Camping: Petoskey State Park, Fisherman's Island State Park.
Services: The best of the area's eating and shopping is in Charlevoix, Petoskey, and Harbor Springs, from small cafe's to fine dining. Hotels, motels, and resorts.
Nearby attractions: Traverse City, Tunnel of Trees.

 The drive

Begin this drive in Charlevoix. (You can learn more about Charlevoix in Drive 21.) In the heart of "Charlevoix the Beautiful," follow US 31 North across the Memorial Bridge. Heading east out of town you can see Beaver Island to your left in the expanse of Lake Michigan.

Beaver Island is a simple, plain island with a fascinating history as the only kingdom to ever exist within the borders of the United States. A Mormon leader named James Jesse Strang brought two thousand followers to the island in the 1850s and declared the piece of land his own private kingdom, appointing himself nothing less than king. When Strang and his group arrived, the island was already inhabited by villages of Irish fishermen. The Mormon followers took over the island, which was not hard to do because they had the power of numbers behind them, and drove the fishermen away. Shortly after that, Strang was killed by a Mormon rebel and the fishermen reclaimed their village.

You can visit Beaver Island by ferry, either taking a day trip or staying at one of the small resorts or camping facilities. This island lacks the gloss of neighbor Charlevoix, but many people prefer it because of its rugged charm.

Drive 20: Charlevoix to Harbor Springs

Petoskey and Bay View

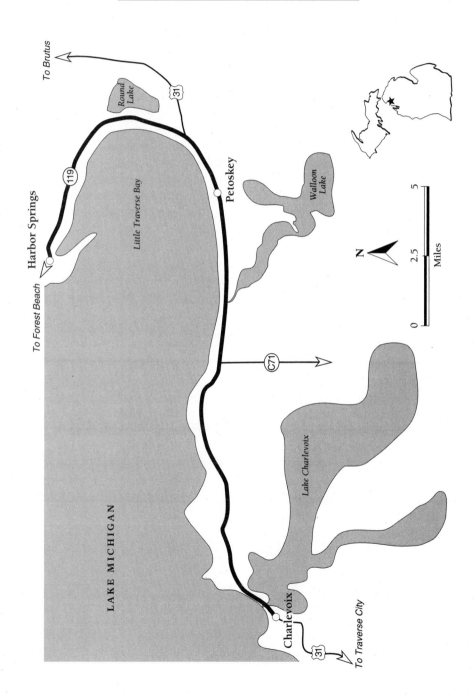

As you are heading out of town, US 31 is also called Struthers Road. Follow it approximately 8 miles to Nine Mile Point, a boat launch, which is to your left.

As you follow the road for about another 3 miles you will come to CR 71. Continue past this intersection traveling east on US 31, which here is called Charlevoix Road. You will have long windswept shores greeting you to your left.

Proceeding north, you round the east cove of Little Traverse Bay, and after about 3.5 miles come into a medium sized resort town called Petoskey. Petoskey is a charming town that has staved off some of the higher-end developments that have been built in neighboring resort towns like Charlevoix and Harbor Springs. As you enter Petoskey, you will cross the Bear River which pours into Little Traverse Bay.

In 1879, when timber was diminishing by great amounts, the railroad and local lumber industries began promoting this area as a resort town. Since then, it has been a summer paradise for some of the wealthiest families in the midwest.

The area was named for the Petoskey Stone. Commonly found in this area, *Hexagonaria percarinata* is actually fossilized coral. It was made the official stone of Michigan in 1965. The Petoskey Stone's orignation can be traced back as far as 350 million years. As glaciers moved across the Great

Pier at Harbor Springs.

Lakes region, they scraped the surface. Fragments of this rock were broken away from the Devonian formations, mixed around, and distributed throughout the area. These rocks appear gray, round, smooth, and nonspecific at first glance. To tell if you have found a Petoskey stone you must immerse it in water. When wet, it will show honey-comb markings, which tell the story of the compressed coral.

Following the highway east through town, you will come to a series of parks to your left, next to the water's edge. You will find Bayfront Park to your right, at the mouth of the Bear River which splashes and spins its way into Lake Michigan. The Bayfront Park Resource Center here notes the history of the region. The park also has a playground and picnic area.

Petoskey is famous for the Gaslight District in its Victorian downtown. Splendid storefronts and well preserved cottages line the shopping area that has been catering to tourists for more than one hundred years.

Proceeding out of Petoskey you come to the Methodist Association of Bay View, located on your right. Bay View, just north of Petoskey, was built before the 1900s as a place for Methodist summer camp meetings. These cottages boast large gingerbread cutouts and Queen Anne design. As you drive through the area it is hard to believe that Bay View started out as a tent camp and grew into these elaborate homes. This area also includes a hotel, chapel, and library.

Summer cottage in Bay View, originally created as a Methodist summer colony.

As the first formal summer colony in the northwoods of Michigan, Bay View is built on natural ledges that formed near the lake's edge during post-glacial times. You can take a sidetrip through Bay View by turning right on Fairview Avenue. From there just meander around the side streets and absorb the stunning cottages and beautiful designs. Bay View is primarily unoccupied during the winter months.

Heading out of Bay View on MI 22, turn left on MI 119. Proceed about 2 miles to the entrance of Petoskey State Park. This is a small beautiful park of only 305 acres. Petoskey State Park offers a soft sandy beach, camping, and picnic areas. Not only is this a good spot to hunt for Petoskey stones, but the blend of hardwoods mixed with towering pine trees makes for a brilliant autumn display.

As you leave Petoskey State Park, head north on MI 119 around the curve of Little Traverse Bay for about 5 miles until you reach the outskirts of Harbor Springs, a bustling, high-end tourist mecca. You will find a visit to this splendid town a step back in time, when elegance and fun were partners. For more detailed information on Harbor Springs, see Drive 19.

21

Traverse City To Charlevoix
Northwest Coast of Lower Peninsula

General description: This 50-mile drive begins in Traverse City, filled with brightly colored cottages, blue sweeping beaches, and orchards full of cherry trees. It ends in another vacation hotspot, Charlevoix, with its wonderful parks, long and lazy beaches, and fine restaurants.

Special attractions: Traverse City is brimming with things to do and places to see, including the Malabar, the Music House, Petobego State Game Area, Con Foster Museum, and Acme Township Park.

Location: Along the northwest edge of the lower peninsula.

Drive route numbers: Michigan Highway 72, and U.S. Highway 31.

Travel season: Year-round, busiest time is height of summer. The crowds can make driving through the towns difficult and frustrating.

Camping: Fisherman's Island State Park in Charlevoix.

Services: Traverse City and Charlevoix cater to the traveler. They probably have anything you might want or need.

Nearby attractions: Sleeping Dunes National Lakeshore, The Dune Climb, Ironton Ferry south of Charlevoix, and Beaver Island.

 The drive

Begin in Traverse City, a large town nestled in the south cove of Grand Traverse Bay's West End Arm. A slick, trendy resort area, this tourist mecca has its roots in the lumber and fur trades that depended upon the nearby waterways and woods.

The drive unfolds into spectacular resort beauty. There are brightly colored cottages, beaches as blue as those in the Carribean, and row after row of petite, wispy cherry trees. The Traverse City of today, with its blend of Victorian homes and storefronts, trendy restaurants, espresso bars, and gift shops, is quite different from the rugged fur trade and lumber empire it was years ago.

Before any white men settled in the Grand Traverse Bay region, this area was a prime meeting and hunting place of the "three brothers"—the Ottawa, Ojibwe, and Potawatomi Indians. They were called "three brothers" because they were quite friendly with one another over the course of many years. Archaeologists have found six burial grounds here, as well as

Drive 21: Traverse City To Charlevoix
Northwest Coast of Lower Peninsula

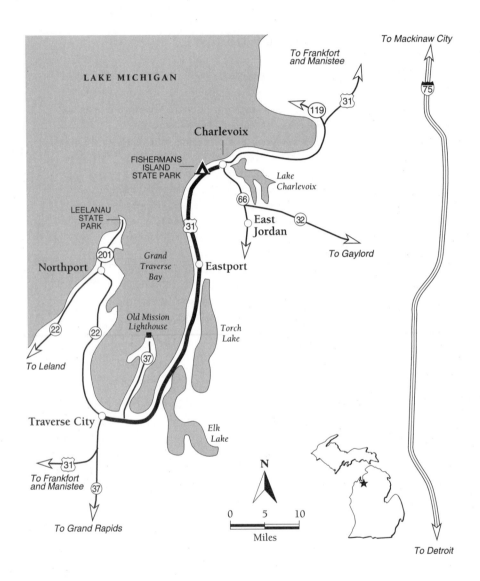

To Mackinaw City

To Frankfort
and Manistee

LAKE MICHIGAN

75

119 31

Charlevoix

FISHERMANS
ISLAND
STATE PARK

Lake
Charlevoix

66

East
Jordan

32

To Gaylord

LEELANAU
STATE
PARK

201

31

Northport

Grand
Traverse
Bay

Eastport

22

22

Old Mission
Lighthouse

Torch
Lake

37

To Leland

Traverse City

Elk
Lake

31

To Frankfort
and Manistee

37

To Grand Rapids

N

0   5   10

Miles

To Detroit

the sites of at least eight Indian villages.

However, some of the earliest explorations of this area date back to 1641, when subjects of the King of France came through this area intent on extending France's power into America. It was the French who named this area *la grande traverse*, which means "the long crossing."

Grand Traverse County had a population of 8,422 in 1880. At last count, the population was over 131,000. Settling began in the spring of 1839, when Reverand Peter Dougherty was sent to this area by Henry Rowe Schoolcraft, an Indian agent stationed at Sault Ste. Marie.

This region was a hub for logging activity. Lumberjacks flocked to the area, and the very first sawmill was constructed here in 1847. It was built by Horace Boardman and located at the head of the West Bay. The population began to increase around the mill's location. Boardman ran his mill until 1851, when he sold it to Perry Hannah, A.T. Lay, and James and William Morgan, who founded Hannah, Lay and Company. A larger mill was then erected and run until 1914.

You can reach Traverse City in one of many ways. MI 72 passes through town from the east or west. If you are coming from the south, take Michigan Highway 37, also labeled US 31, right into the heart of town.

Begin the drive where MI 72 and US 31 meet at the bay. Head east on US 31 past several beaches, which are to your left. Nestled in the protected cove of the bay, area beaches include West End Beach, Clinch Park Beach, and Bryant Park Beach. All offer swimming, piers for fishing, and boat launches.

You may also see the *Malabar*, a 105-foot ship, one of the largest sailing rigs on the Great Lakes. The *Malabar* also functions as a floating bed and breakfast. This old-time clipper ship tours shore villages and islands. Also located on the waterfront is the Con Foster Museum which gives in-depth geological and historical information about how the area was formed.

As you pass the beaches, follow US 31 north. Pass MI 37 leading to Old Mission Peninsula (see Drive 17). Continue past East Bay Beach to your left, and 0.5 miles later you will come to Traverse City State Park, on your left. Both East Bay Beach and Traverse City State Park offer great swimming in the secure hamlet of the East Arm of Grand Traverse Bay.

Proceeding north on US 31, you will come to the Music House at mile 3. The Music House is an old granary built in 1905 that showcases musical instruments made from 1880 to 1920. You'll find everything here from the tiniest of music boxes to the largest and grandest ballroom organs.

After about 3.5 miles, the drive enters lovely rolling pastures and cherry orchards. Soil here is perfect for cultivating this crop, an important part of the area economy. Traverse City hosts the National Cherry Festival, which takes place each July. In 1923, the festival was preceded by a Sunday church

Overlook of the marina at Traverse City.

service called "The Blessing of the Blossoms." This simple service was offered out in the orchards where the residents of the region were asked to come and pray for a successful harvest.

As you drive through this agricultural region another 5.5 miles, you reach Acme Township Park, a soft, sandy beach for swimming and camping. The park is located to your left, on the shore of Lake Michigan.

Proceed north on US 31. After another 5 miles, you pass through an area called Petobego State Game Area, which is partially a wetland. This area is home to muskrat, rabbit, deer, and mink. Mink are fierce animals and prone to snarly temper tantrums. They are excellent swimmers, and prefer to live near water. The mink was once hunted to great extent for its valued silky fur.

For the next couple of miles, you near the shore of the bay to your left, allowing a good view of Lake Michigan's deep blue waters. About 18 miles into the trip, you come into the town of Elk Rapids. This area was discovered in 1846 by settler Abraham Wadsworth, who eventually was responsible for creating the town.

During the mid-1800s, the lumber companies were harvesting great amounts of white pine in this area to help rebuild Chicago after the devastating Great Chicago Fire. The lumber industry flourished and grand Victorian homes appeared, built mostly by lumber barons of Elk Rapids and Bellaire. As the lumber industry dwindled in the early the 1900s, Elk Rapids became all but a ghost town. In an effort to revitalize the economy, settlers used the cleared lands as farmland. Many of these farmers used post-Civil War homestead rights to obtain land. You can spot some of these older homes and farms as you proceed north.

In about 2 miles, you pass Birch Lake to your right and have beautiful bay views to your left. After another mile, you cross Paradine Creek, a thin trickling bed of water which flows into Lake Michigan. Proceeding north about 4 miles through apple orchards, you come to the town of Torch Lake. This town is situated on the western shore of Torch Lake, which you can see to your right. At this location, you are at the upper one-third of this long, narrow lake, which extends about 14 miles to the south.

Proceeding north another 1.5 miles, as you near the end of Torch Lake, you come in to the town of Eastport. The elevation of the road rises here with the hills of pine and cedar forests. Six miles past Eastport, apple orchards again line the roadside.

After about 10 miles, portions of Fisherman's Island State Park appear to your left, between the road and Lake Michigan. The main entrance to this unspoiled park is 2 miles south of Charlevoix. This 3,000-acre area was converted from state forest to state park in 1978, and is the closest state park to Charlevoix.

As you approach Charlevoix, touted as "Charlevoix the Beautiful," turn left on Bell's Bay Road to the entrance of the park. This park has ninety campsites, a scenic overlook, rock and sand formed beaches, and an uncrowded atmosphere. This area is also a hotbed for rockhounders searching for Petoskey stones—broken pieces of compressed coral.

Many walking paths meander through the surrounding hardwood trees. Because this is a low, moist area, the forests are a combination of spruce, tamarack, and balsam fir trees. The park is open from May until November.

Leaving the park, take Bell's Bay Road back to US 31 and turn left toward Charlevoix. At the crest of the hill you are greeted by a sweeping view of Lake Michigan, punctuated by sailboats, schooners, and fishing boats. Charlevoix County was named after Pierre Francois-Xavier de Charlevoix. An undercover agent for the French, he was assigned the task of determining the existence of a northwest passage.

It is easy to see why this area is called "Charelvoix the Beautiful." This small town is situated on three lakes—Lake Michigan, Lake Charlevoix, and Round Lake. Resort traffic and tourism give this town its character. This city, including the surrounding townships, has a total population of about 8,500 people year-round. However, that number explodes to over twenty thousand during the summer months. Many local residents avoid the busy downtown area during peak times. Sleeper times to visit are late spring or fall.

As you enter Charlevoix, the hustle and bustle is noticeable. This is a resort haven for those who can afford the dual allure of Lake Charlevoix and Lake Michigan. Quaint small-town shops geared to the high-end tourist line the main street. To your right is a cozy harbor filled with expensive boats. Condos line the edges of the harbor.

You can drive through the middle of town and follow Memorial Bridge which spans the Pine River Channel, the waterway connecting Round Lake to Lake Michigan. The Pine River was dredged during the logging years to form this channel so lumber boats could pass easily between the lakes. This is a bascule bridge, which means it can open at the midsection and each half is hinged at the end. Though the bridge is charming, it causes traffic delays when it opens for boats during peak season.

22

East Arm of Traverse Bay
Old Mission Peninsula

General description: An astounding 20-mile drive in a pastoral setting from Traverse City to the tip of the Old Mission Peninsula.
Special attractions: The beautiful farms, orchards, wineries, beaches, Old Mission Point Lighthouse and Old Mission, and Bowers Harbor.
Location: The northwest portion of the lower peninsula.
Drive route numbers: Michigan Highway 37, Peninsula Drive.
Travel season: Year-round.
Camping: In nearby Traverse City.
Services: Full services in Traverse City. Quaint cafes, little shops, and galleries along the drive.
Nearby attractions: Traverse City, Pere Marquette State Forest, Clinch Park Zoo, the Music House.

 # The drive

It is about 20 miles from Traverse City to the tip of Old Mission Peninsula, which separates Grand Traverse Bay into two portions—the East Arm and the West Arm. This drive to Old Mission Point and back on MI 37 will take you through rich cherry and wine country. The water of the beaches in the well-protected West Arm of Grand Traverse Bay is blue as a cornflower, serving up glimpses of soft white sand beneath the waves.

Begin this drive by following MI 37 north out of Traverse City. This is the doorstep to Old Mission Peninsula. You will notice that MI 37 splits into two roads: Peninsula Drive, which goes to the west and hugs the shore, and MI 37 which travels midway through the peninsula. At this point, stay to the right on MI 37. You will travel on Peninsula Drive on the return trip.

After about 2.5 miles, you crest over a small hill and are exposed to views of Lake Michigan on both sides of the road. You are actually driving on a finger of land that extends into Lake Michigan. This portion of the drive features long, pastoral scenery dotted with farms and a few residences.

This region has a strong presence in the fruit market. When Reverend Peter Dougherty arrived on this peninsula in the 1800s, he found apple trees which had been planted from seed. He concluded that the apple trees had been planted by the Indians, who used apples as an item to trade with other villages. When early white families arrived, they planted fruit for pri-

Drive 22: East Arm of Traverse Bay

Old Mission Peninsula

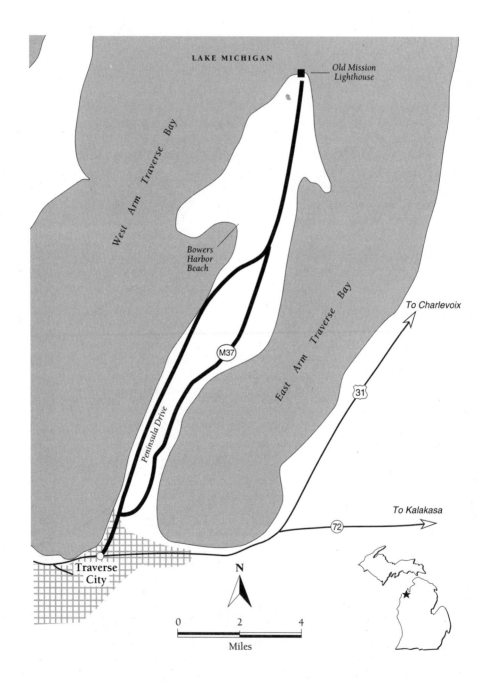

LAKE MICHIGAN

West Arm Traverse Bay

Old Mission Lighthouse

Bowers Harbor Beach

East Arm Traverse Bay

M37

To Charlevoix

31

Peninsula Drive

To Kalakasa

72

Traverse City

N

0   2   4

Miles

vate consumption. They learned that apples and cherries did very well in this soil, and since then the area has become known for its fruit. Eventually, it was learned that grapes could do well in this soil, too, and that was the catalyst for the many wineries located in this region.

Hill after hill and orchard after orchard, you are exposed to sweeping panoramas at every crest and fall. Orchard trees are neatly arranged in rows, and when in blossom during the spring, have a delicate and frilly appearance. Grape vines hang thick, with bright hues of green.

Proceeding north, after driving another 1.5 miles, you arrive at the East Arm Public Access. The water here is a brilliant blue-green, and so clear that, even from the road, you can see directly to the sandy bottom. As you crest up and away from the lake into cherry orchards lined with maple trees, you can see why this area is a favorite among people trying to "get away from it all."

After driving a total of about 8 miles, you rise along a small hill again and, through grape vines, see Lake Michigan and its sandy shores to your left. The vineyard is between the road and the lake, soaking up the lake-tempered climate.

Continuing north for several miles there are more orchards, and the road is lined with hardwood trees. You can see homes and farms ranging from quaint and traditional to modern and expansive. The road is quite busy at times, especially during cherry harvest season which takes place in mid-summer. There are roadside stands that sell brown bags plump with cherries. Watch out for stopped cars on the narrow shoulder here.

About 6 miles after the vineyard, the road turns sharply west for about 1 mile. Then it takes you about 2.5 miles to the northwest edge of the peninsula, right along the lakeshore. Sunbathers take full advantage of the sunny beaches, while breezy sailboats raise their sails in the winds and whisk by.

You'll find Lighthouse Park in another 0.5 mile near the tip of the peninsula, at the end of MI 37. You can reach the park by driving through thick rows of hardwood trees, which are beautiful during autumn. You will see Old Mission Lighthouse standing at the uppermost edge of the peninsula. This park lighthouse was built in the 1870 and stands exactly on the 45th parallel, which is equidistant from the North Pole and the Equator.

As you return, take MI 37 south from the parking lot of the lighthouse. Travel about 2 miles, then turn left on Swaney Road and follow it to the small village of Old Mission. The village is located in a snug hamlet called Old Mission Harbor on the upper east edge of the peninsula. It was here that education in Grand Traverse County got underway.

It was the fall of 1853, and a schooner called *Madeline* dropped anchor in the harbor. There were four men aboard, William Bryce, Edward Chambers, and two brothers with the last name Fitzgerald. These men were intent on wintering nearby. They decided to use their spare time during the long

Roadside stands offer beautiful baskets of fruit along the Old Mission Peninsula drive.

winter to improve upon their knowledge. They hired a young man named S. E. Whittier Wait, a resident of Old Mission, to tutor them. It was before the first snowfall that the *Madeline* was moved about 6 miles south and to the other side of the peninsula into a well-protected cove now called Bowers Harbor. This was the beginning of Grand Traverse County's educational system. A plaque still stands at Bowers Harbor denoting it as such.

While you are in Old Mission, visit Haserot Beach with its 250 feet of sand and rock. This area is protected from harsh winds and is busy during the summer. There is also the Old Mission Museum, a replica of the log mission built when Presbyterian missionaries came to this area in the 1800s.

As you leave Old Mission, travel west on Swaney Road back to MI 37. Proceed south for about 5 miles until you come to a fork in the road. Stay to your right, which is Peninsula Drive. Penninsula Drive takes you west to Bowers Harbor, the location of the plaque describing the start of Grand Traverse County's educational system. Bowers Harbor Inn is a great place for Sunday brunch during the summer.

Back on MI 37 going south, the road hugs the west shore and, to your right, you will have splendid views of Lake Michigan's West Arm of Grand Traverse Bay. Follow the remainder of the road south to Traverse City. You will have lovely rolling cherry farms to your left and Lake Michigan to your right all the way back. See Drive 21 for detailed information on Traverse City.

A seemingly tropical beach on the shore of Traverse Bay's East Arm.

23

Frankfort to Suttons Bay

Sleeping Bear Dunes National Lakeshore and Leelanau Peninsula

General description: This 66-mile drive from Frankfort to Suttons Bay takes you through towering sand dunes that loom hundreds of feet high. The Sleeping Bear Dunes National Lakeshore is one of the most popular tourist attractions in the state of Michigan. This drive leads you along the coast of Lake Michigan, north through small fishing towns, recreation areas, and through the Leelanau Peninsula.
Special attractions: Dune Climb, Platte River Point.
Location: The northwest portion of the lower peninsula.
Drive route numbers: Michigan Highway 22 and Michigan Highway 109.
Travel season: Year-round.
Camping: North and South Manitou Island, D. H. Day Campground, Leelanau State Park South, and Leelanau State Park at the tip of the peninsula.
Services: Frankfort has full services. There are a few restaurants along the way near Platte River. Empire has full sevices, scattered restaurants. There is fine shopping at many spots.
Nearby attractions: Crystal River, Interlochen Center for the Arts.

 The drive

Frankfort and its neighbor to the south, Ludington, each have markers paying tribute to Father Jacques Marquette. The actual location of his death has remained a mystery, but it is believed that when he died in May of 1675, he was buried somewhere along the western shore of the lower peninsula, most likely in either Frankfort or Ludington.

Start this drive at MI 22 heading north out of Frankfort. You can reach it by heading north on Michigan Avenue or Bellows Road and turning left onto MI 22. The road will then immediately cling to the shore of Crystal Lake, to your right.

After 1.5 miles, you will pass the Betsie Point Lighthouse on your left. This structure was built in 1858. To access it for a closer view, turn left on Point Betsie Road.

Resume your direction north on MI 22, and stay to your right as the

Drive 23: Frankfort to Suttons Bay

Sleeping Bear Dunes National Lakeshore and Leelanau Peninsula

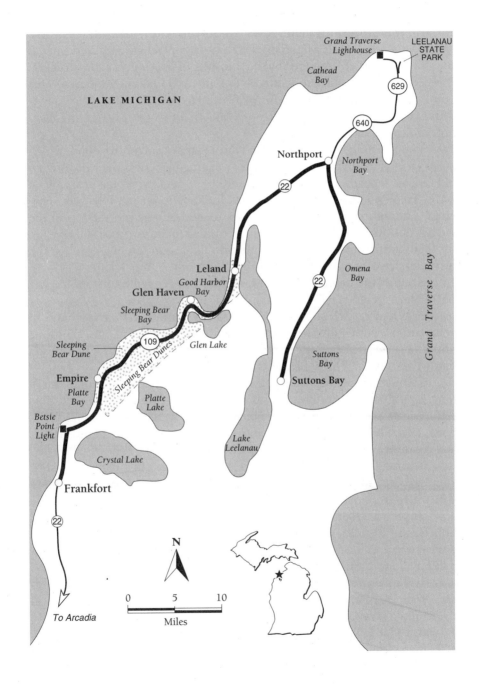

road veers toward the shore of Crystal Lake's Winetka Point. Follow MI 22 as it rounds the point, and then proceed north. About 4 miles into the drive, you will come to the intersection of MI 22 and Sutter Road. Turn right. Here, the road becomes Pine Highway. Follow it for a few miles to Lake Michigan Road. Turn left.

As you proceed to Platte River Point, you will notice a thick marsh area to your left. This is a good place to spot trumpeter swans gliding across the still pools which are edged by the soft sway of tall cattails and bulrushes. Proceed west for 2 miles to Platte River Point and Platte River Beach. This point gives you wonderful views of Platte Bay and Sleeping Bear Dunes National Lakeshore. The Platte River is known for its great swimming, fishing, and canoeing.

The Sleeping Bear Dune is the world's largest migrating dune, which means it is always moving. The name "sleeping bear" was derived from an old Ojibwe legend of a mother bear and her two cubs. As the bears swam across Lake Michigan to escape a forest fire in Wisconsin, they were separated. The mother bear reached the shore, and climbed to the top of the highest dune to await her cubs' return. According to the story, she still watches for them in the form of the black mound that sits on top of the dune. The lost cubs have become known as the North and South Manitou islands, sitting out in the depths of Lake Michigan. The rugged bluffs of Sleeping Bear Dunes are 460 feet above Lake Michigan.

Back out on MI 22 North, you pass the Platte River campground to your left. To your right are Platte Lake and Little Platte Lake. Continue north for several miles along the scenic lakeshore, poking your way through hardwood trees and hills, nearing the vicinity of Empire.

A few miles before you reach Empire, the road begins to undulate in long, lazy hills. Look for meadows dotted with apple trees on your left. This setting is as serene as an impressionistic painting with its pastoral backdrop, edged by white pine and cedar trees, accentuated with farm homes and pastures.

The road pitches to the right and left, and signs will direct you to slow your speed to forty-five miles per hour. The road quickly becomes dense with foliage from hardwood trees. Empire, a small town that does have some services such as restaurants, gas, and motels, is in a deep valley of lush thick hills. About 15 miles into the drive, you will reach the visitor center for the dunes, which is located in Empire. This is a great place to stop to get information about the area and its massive, sweeping mounds of sand.

Two miles out of Empire you pass the entrance to Pierce Stocking Scenic Drive (See Drive 24). Proceed north through the dunes and you will come into heavy sands to your left and Glen Lake to your right.

In about 1.5 miles, you will come to the intersection of MI 22 and MI 109. Turn right and follow MI 22. Proceed straight to Glen Haven and Glen

Shoreline near Glen Harbor on the Sleeping Bear Dunes National Lakeshore.

Haven Beach. You will notice a large red storage building that was once a canning factory. This is the parking area for the beach, so park next to the building.

To resume the drive, leave the beach area and proceed back to the intersection of MI 22 and MI 109. Turn right (north) on MI 109. You will pass D. H. Day Campground to your left as you edge the shore of Sleeping Bear Bay. D. H. Day Campground, situated on a piece of land created by a post-glacial sandbar, has many campsites.

As you continue north on MI 22, you may notice wild turkeys lurking along the roadsides. The wild turkey is characterized by its long tail with black band near the tip. The male turkey is shiny brown with a bare head and trademark red wattle and can grow to four feet long from head to tail. Females are typically smaller and not as brightly colored.

Continue through the dunes, passing Good Harbor Beach and Good Harbor Bay, to your left. This area is home to the prairie warbler, a threatened Michigan species that is frequent here in May and June. The prairie warbler has an olive colored back and a yellow belly, as well as black spots along its sides. The prairie warbler avoids dense forest, opting to inhabit areas with young seedlings and small bushes.

As you head north on MI 22, you begin to enter the Leelanau Peninsula. This peninsula is referred to as the little finger of the mitten-shaped lower peninsula. This little piece of land extends 30 miles into Lake Michigan, which forms the west arm of Grand Traverse Bay. This piece of land was formed by a glacier. As the glacier retreated north, it created formations called "drumlins" in its wake. A drumlin is a long, streamlined hill.

The first settlements here were three Ojibwe and Ottawa Indian missions built south of Northport during the years 1849 to 1852. Protestant missionaries brought Indians to this area because they thought it was somewhat isolated and tucked away from the negative influences and corruption of white settlers and fur traders.

About 6 miles north of Good Harbor Beach, you pass Good Harbor Vineyard on your right. At 6.5 miles you will pass through a slim fit of land that exposes Lake Michigan to the left and Lake Leelanau to the right.

After another 1.5 miles you will pass through the quaint town of Leland, located on the piece of land between the two bodies of water. Continue traveling north on MI 22 for about 13 miles until you reach Northport. For a pleasant side trip from Northport, turn left on MI 201 and proceed north 10 miles to Leelanau State Park, home of the Grand Traverse Light. The Light is a beautiful lighthouse situated on a sandy, pebbled shore. Leelanau State Park is 1,200 acres with 52 beautiful campsites, most reserved well in advance. There is also a park, beach, and lighthouse museum. Once you have returned to Northport, turn right on MI 22 heading south. This portion of the highway hugs the west coast of the peninsula, traveling along Northport Bay, which is now to your left.

As you proceed south along the shore, you will be passing through vineyard country, charcterized by rolling pastures filled with vines, fences, wineries, and homes. Continue south along the shore until you reach Suttons Bay.

Suttons Bay was initially prosperous from the success of sawmills, and the area eventually saw success from the fruit-growing industry. In the 1970s, this area started to attract artisans and craftspeople trying to escape the hectic pace of city life. Here, you will find trendy gift shops, art studios, galleries, and coffee shops. Traffic is quite congested during the summer months, so be prepared to be patient. The town is well worth the wait for good food and hotels.

24

Pierce Stocking Scenic Drive

General description: This drive is a 7.5-mile loop through sweeping dunescapes, and ghost forests, with panoramic views of Lake Michigan.
Special attractions: The entire drive is filled with overlooks of the Sleeping Bear Dunes Area.
Location: The northwest portion of the lower peninsula.
Drive route numbers: Michigan Highway 109, Pierce Stocking Scenic Drive.
Travel season: Year-round, but check with visitor's center about road conditions during winter.
Camping: D. H. Day Campground nearby, but none on drive.
Services: Full services in Empire.
Nearby attractions: Dune Climb, Sleeping Bear Dunes National Lakeshore.

 The drive

Pierce Stocking Scenic Drive is a 7.5-mile loop at Sleeping Bear Dunes National Lakeshore which takes you from sweeping dunescapes to bird's-eye views of Lake Michigan, through forests of beech, maple, and pine trees. This short drive is packed with information and natural wonders. You can pick up brochures that describe the area in fine detail at the Sleeping Bear Dunes Visitor Center in Empire.

The drive is named after Pierce Stocking, a Michigan lumberman and nature lover. Stocking labored in the forests of Michigan as a young man, appreciating nature and acquiring knowledge about the land. He enjoyed the sweeping views from the top of the dunes and always imagined a road there. In the 1960s, planning for such a road began. In 1967, the road was created as part of a visitor's attraction called Sleeping Bear Dunes Park. Pierce Stocking operated the drive until his death in 1976. In 1977, this road became part of the Sleeping Bear Dunes National Lakeshore, and several years later the drive was re-named Pierce Stocking Scenic Drive.

The best way to find the Pierce Stocking Scenic Drive is by traveling north out of Empire on MI 109. If you are coming to Empire from the east, travel on US 2 West. From the south, MI 22 will take you into town, where you can pick up MI 109.

Drive 24: Pierce Stocking Scenic Drive

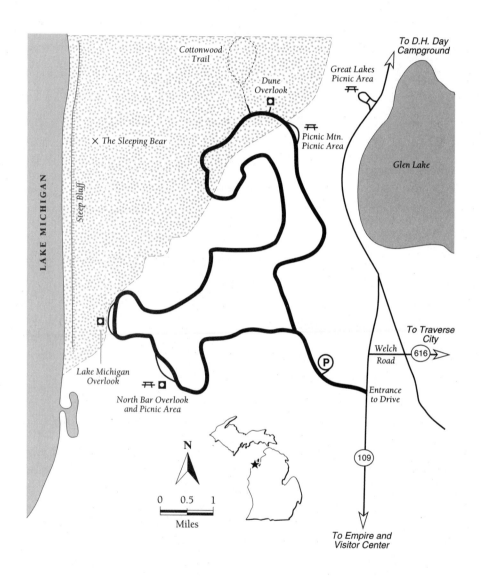

Cottonwood Trail

Dune Overlook

Great Lakes Picnic Area

To D.H. Day Campground

Picnic Mtn. Picnic Area

× The Sleeping Bear

Glen Lake

LAKE MICHIGAN

Steep Bluff

To Traverse City

616

Welch Road

Lake Michigan Overlook

Entrance to Drive

North Bar Overlook and Picnic Area

N

0   0.5   1

Miles

109

To Empire and Visitor Center

Follow MI 109 north to Pierce Stocking Scenic Drive. The area is well marked and you will see signs directing you to turn left. When you turn into the drive entrance, you will notice signs designating the 20 MPH speed limit. Take this seriously. The road is open to walkers, hikers, bicycles, and motorcyles, as well as wandering animals.

Once you turn into the scenic drive area, parking is to your right. If you are interested in exploring the drive by bicycle or foot, park there and let your adventure begin.

As you start onto the Drive, the road is two-way for about 0.5 mile. You will then follow the road to your right and it becomes a one-way loop.

At 0.5 mile, you pass beneath a quaint covered bridge. The original covered bridge, a wooden structure, had side panels that were eaten by porcupines, who must have thought it a treat. There is a pulloff if you wish to take pictures or explore the romance of a covered bridge.

After another 1.5 miles, you come to the beautiful blue waters of Glen Lake and Little Glen Lake. This is a lake in two parts, divided by a constriction at the narrows. Little Glen Lake is shallow, only 12 feet deep at its deepest point. Glen Lake is much bigger and 130 feet deep in its far reaches. It is believed that the larger Glen Lake was linked to Lake Michigan until a post-glacial sandbar created a barrier. On this sandbar now sit the D. H. Day Campground and the village of Glen Arbor.

You can pull off here and ponder the sweeping vistas. To your north is "Alligator Hill." The name refers to the hill's shape, created by early post-glacial movement. As the glacier melted and began to retreat, it carried sediment of sand, soil, and rock to re-deposit along its path. Much of the hilly terrain derives from this post-glacial affect.

Back on the Drive, you will come to the Dune Overlook after about 2 miles. From the top of 200-foot dunes you will get an incredible view of Sleeping Bear, Pyramid Point, and Glen Lake. You will also be able to see the Little Glen Lake Mill Pond and D. H. Day Farm. Expansive, this view is best when you are standing at the eastern edge of the dunes. As you look into the deep lake, you also see South and North Manitou islands. The waterspan between the mainland and the islands, the Manitou Passage, has an interesting history.

In the eary 1900s, many shipping vessels—up to one hundred per day—would pass through this area because it was considered a shortcut. However, the shallow reef-like shoals and slim passageway prevented many of these ships from completing safe passage. The area saw many shipwrecks.

Proceed back out to the road. One half mile later, you will notice the Cottonwood Trail to your right. You can access a trailhead that offers a 1.5 mile walk along the dunescape. You will notice areas of sparse vegetation (bearberry and buffaloberry) that root in this dunescape. The bearberry can grow up to ten feet long, and sport a whitish-pink urn-shaped bloom. Small bunches of reddish purple berries adorn this plant, one of many that thrive in dry, sandy soil. The large cavities you see at this point are called "blow-outs"—divots that have been hollowed out by strong winds.

As you continue to drive, you will begin to notice cottonwood trees. Cottonwoods are common here in the sand of the dunes because they survive the least desirable of conditions like low soil fertility, driving winds, and deep soil erosions. The cottonwood grows quickly, keeping ahead of the strong winds and migrating dunes. They also tend to grow in clusters because their roots send up new shoots, which results in additional trees. These clusters, in turn, stabilize the surrounding sand, which actually helps other plant life maintain a hold in the dunes.

In about 1 mile, you will reach a forest of beech and maple trees. Sugar maple and American beech trees dominate this forest, while other hardwoods, such as hemlock and basswood trees mingle in the understory. This beech and maple climax forest has survived because the trees are shade tolerant. That is, they can survive beneath a dense understory of mature trees, which gives them a chance to reach the canopy and become part of the overstory. As the canopy grows dense, shade intolerant trees are not able to withstand the lack of sun and, therefore, do not survive long enough to mature. Eventually, the entire forest becomes filled with the beech and maple trees.

Twists and turns along the Pierce Stocking Drive.

This kind of environment is good for catching glimpses of wildlife such as whitetail deer, squirrels, and wood thrushes. Characterized by a red-brown back and a head with large brown spots, the wood thrush, or *Hylocichla mustelina*, favors a habitat rich in moist deciduous trees. The mud-lined nest of a wood thrush is small, and almost cup shaped. You can tell if you are near a wood thrush by the softly muted "pip-pip-pip" echoing through the forest.

In autumn, this part of the drive is like harvest-colored confetti, with yellow beech trees tangled amid the scarlet shades of maple trees. About 5 miles into this drive is an overlook 450 feet above Lake Michigan. Exposed to the massive sweeping sight of Empire Bluffs and Platte Bay, the shoreline seems infinite. If the weather is clear, you might even see Point Betsie, 15 miles away.

Peering down the slope of this bluff you can see layers of sand and rock. This is actually a glacial hill, not a sand dune. This outcropping has been eroding for years, as much as one foot per year. Erosion occurs from the repetitive pounding action of Lake Michigan waves, which eventually destabilize the base, prompting portions of the upper hill to fall off.

To the right of the Lake Michigan overlook is the Sleeping Bear Dune Overlook. Sleeping Bear Dune is estimated to be over two thousand years old. Because this dune is sitting on top of a plateau, it is referred to as a perched dune. The Sleeping Bear Dune was formed by sand-carrying winds that blew in from the upper portion of the Lake Michigan bluff. From here, you spy haunting remnants of what is called a ghost forest. The dark, sharp spires poking through the sand are skeletons of trees that were buried by migrating sand dunes. Eventually, the moving sand swirls away and the dead trees are left barren and exposed.

At one time, this dune was more than 234 feet high and covered with dense plant life. Erosion has caused the dune to shrink; it was measured at 103 feet in 1980. As waves wear away at its base and top portions continue to weaken, it will only be a matter of time until this great dune disappears forever.

As you head back out on the scenic loop, you are traveling toward the end of the Drive. North Bar Lake is about 0.5 mile away, on your right. North Bar Lake is a product of the quick changing terrain in Sleeping Dunes National Park. Formed as a pool behind a sand bar, there are times when the sandbar builds up so high that it actually separates this small lake from Lake Michigan. Other times, a channel exists between the two.

Rounding your way back to the parking lot, you travel through a stand of pine trees created when property owners tried to replace the trees lost to logging and farming. The trees were planted before the area became part of the National Lakeshore. They seem a bit out of place in an environment that is otherwise natural. To help encourage a natural environ, some sections of the pine plantation have been cut to encourage the growth of natural trees.

Proceeding back toward the parking lot, continue straight to the park exit. From there, you can turn right onto MI 109 and head south to Empire, or turn left onto MI 109 and proceed north along the Sleeping Bear Dunes National Lakeshore. To learn more about the National Lakeshore, see Drive 23.

25

Frankfort to Ludington

General description: This drive from Frankfort to Ludington, approximately 60 miles, follows the west coast of the lower peninsula southward, past sugar sand beaches and the Victorian city of Manistee.
Special attractions: Betsie River State Game Area, Orchard Beach State Park, Manistee, Nordhouse Dunes, Big Sable Point Lighthouse, and Ludington State Park.
Location: The mid-western coast of the lower peninsula.
Drive route numbers: Michigan Highway 22, U.S. Highway 31.
Travel season: Year-round.
Camping: Orchard Beach State Park, Nordhouse Dunes (with some restrictions), Ludington State Park.
Services: Full services the entire drive.
Nearby attractions: Pere Marquette State Forest, Manistee National Forest, Sleeping Bear Dunes National Lakeshore.

 ## The drive

This drive whisks you along the mid-western shore of the lower peninsula through several beach areas and the Victorian port city of Manistee. You can access the drive beginning in Frankfort from County Road 115, which comes in from the east. In Frankfort there are several beaches and watercraft areas, such as Frankfort Municipal Beach, Frankfort North Breakwater Light, and Elberta Municipal Beach.

As you leave Frankfort, head south on Frankfort Avenue, which is also MI 22. Immediately, you round Betsie Lake, to your right. The city and county airport is to your left. Here, CR 608 comes in from the left. Continue straight ahead on MI 22, going south. The road curves here and drops in elevation.

Three miles into the drive, the Betsie River State Game Area is to your left. A large wetland filled with ponds, bogs, and aquatic plants, the Betsie area is similar to Seney National Wildlife Refuge, described in Drive 9.

At mile 6, Upper Herring lake appears in a swampy area to the left. The road continues on through the small town of Arcadia. Continue south, crossing the bridge that spans Arcadia Lake, which pours into Lake Michigan. As you pass the intersection of MI 22 and Chamberlain Road, MI 22 becomes

Drive 25: Frankfort to Ludington

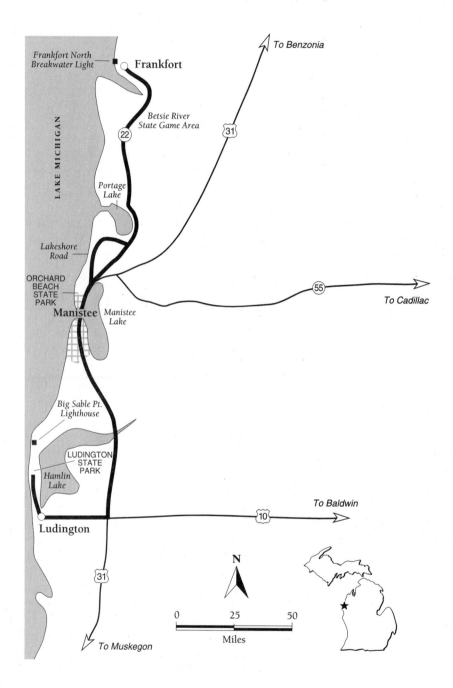

Northwood Highway. Continue on the Northwood Highway.

The next 8 miles take you through hills, forest broken up by agricultural areas, and quick views of Lake Michigan to the right. The Northwood Highway joins Portage Point Drive as it veers left. The road is now called Portage Point Drive, or MI 22. The drive now rounds the east end of Portage Lake in Onekama. As you round the lake, the road is briefly called Beach Road. Beach Road proceeds west as MI 22 veers south, to your left. Continue on Beach Road past that intersection, and after you have traveled 1.5 miles, turn left on Lakeshore Road. Proceeding south about 4.5 miles, you will pass Bar Lake Swamp to your right.

About 1.2 miles farther, you come to Orchard Beach State Park on your right. This park has modern campsites, picnic areas, and is situated on a bluff with great views of Lake Michigan. The swimming beach is sandy and soft, perfect for summertime lingering.

Continue south on Lakeshore Road, which is now called CR 110, for about another 2.3 miles to the city of Manistee. Manistee is located between Lake Michigan and Manistee Lake. It is called "Historic Manistee, the Victorian Port City" because of its stunning architecture, which includes Victorian Italianate, French Chateau, Gothic Revival, and Shingle styles.

In the 1860s, Manistee was a major logging and shipping hub, and these elegant mansions sprang up along the city streets, built mostly by

Two car ferries at Ludington.

lumber barons. In 1879, fire destroyed the business district. The city fathers then redesigned the downtown to be closer to the water so that it would be less susceptible to fire.

As you enter Manistee, the waterfront is to your right. Found here are the Fifth Avenue Beach, the Manistee North Pierhead Light, First Street Beach, and the Historical Museum and Old Waterworks. In the heart of Manistee you cross the Manistee River as it flows from Manistee Lake into Lake Michigan. The road at this point merges into US 31.

Drive south from Manistee on US 31 for about 10 miles. Turn right on Lake Michigan Recreation Area Road. Travel 10 miles on this road to Nordhouse Dunes.

Nordhouse Dunes offers 10 miles of trails through wind-shaped mounds of sand. This is dune country! This 4,300-acre park is brimming with wildlife and flowers, while offering a soft touch for the soles of your feet. The beach is more than 3 miles long, and accented by towering dunes. You can camp along the hiking trails here. This is a part of the Lake Michigan Recreation Area, operated by the USDA Forest Service.

A few miles north of Ludington, before you actually get into the heart of the city, is Big Sable Point Lighthouse. Built in 1867, the tower is 112 feet high and was originally made of brick. High winds and extreme weather threatened the stability of the tower, so it was later encased in steel plates.

Back on US 31, proceed south toward Ludington. In 10 miles take a right on US 10 (which is also US 31) into the heart of Ludington. Ludington was named after James Ludington, a lumberman from Milwaukee who was instrumental in refueling the depressed economy of the 1850s.

There is an active light on the waters called the Ludington North Breakwater, which is in downtown Ludington. This tower still guides vessels through the channel which connects this harbor with the Pere Marquette River and Lake Michigan. The Pere Marquette River is 66 miles long and has been designated a National Wild and Scenic River. The beacon for the Ludington North Breakwater made its debut in 1871. During the 1800's there were as many as sixty-seven lumber-carrying ships breaking through the harbor per month. Stately and tall, it stands at the end of the breakwall, and can send its light 19 miles upon the water.

This port is filled with beaches and boat accesses. Also located at this waterfront is the SS *Badger*, a car ferry that travels between Ludington and Manitowac, Wisconsin. As much a tourist attraction as a necessity, this large boat offers history and convenience. More than 410 feet long and able to carry 620 passengers, it was initially launched in 1952.

Once you are in Ludington, a nice side trip is Ludington State Park. Turn right on Lakeshore Drive, and proceed 8 miles north to park entrance. This park has 5,300 acres of virgin conifer and hardwood trees. The area is

The lighthouse at Ludington State Park.

composed of hills, ravines, and lofty dunes. There is a trail system that winds its way 18 miles through the woods and visits the soft sandy dunes. There are three campgrounds here, and some of the park areas are open to hunting and fishing. Check at the visitor center when you arrive.

This ends the drive from Frankfort to Ludington, but from here you can easily take another interesting side trip. Travel 3 miles south of Ludington to the Rose Hawley Museum. This small museum has Indian, farming, and lumber-era artifacts, as well as old Victorian furnishings. You can see White Pine Village, too, which is a nineteenth-century pioneer settlement. In addition, the Mason County Courthouse is here. Dating from 1855, it was the first county seat.

Appendix
For More Information

General Michigan Information

Upper Peninsula Travel and
  Recreation Association
618 Stephenson Avenue
POB 400
Iron Mountain, MI 49801
906-774-5480

West Michigan Tourist Association
136 East Fulton Street
Grand Rapids, MI 49503
616-456-8557

Michigan's Sunrise Side, Inc.
1361 Fletcher Street
National City, MI 48748
517-469-4544

Michigan Historic Preservation
  Network
POB 398
Clarkston, MI 48347
248-625-8181

Michigan Underwater Preserves
  Council
560 N. State Street
St. Ignace, MI 49781
906-643-8717

Drive 1

Huron City Museums
7930 Huron City Road
Port Austin, MI 48467
517-428-4123

Bay County Historical Society
321 Washington Avenue
Bay City, MI 48708
517-893-5733

Bay County Convention and Visitor's
  Bureau
315 14th Street
Bay City, MI 48708
517-893-1222

Greater Port Austin Area Chamber
  of Commerce
POB 274
Port Austin, MI 48467
517-738-7600

Lakeport State Park
7605 Lakeshore Road
Lakeport, MI 48059
810-327-6765

Port Crescent State Park
1775 Port Austin Road
Port Austin, MI 48467
517-738-8663

Albert E. Sleeper State Park
6573 State Park Road
Caseville, MI 48725
517-856-4411

Bay City Recreational Area
3582 State Park Drive
Bay City, MI 48706
517-684-3020

Drive 2

Huron Shores Ranger Station
Oscoda, MI 48750
517-739-0728

Tawas Point State Park
686 Tawas Beach Road
East Tawas, MI 48730
517-362-5041

Drive 3

Jesse Besser Museum
491 Johnson Street
Alpena, MI 49707
517-356-2202

Rogers City Chamber of Commerce
POB 55
Rogers City, MI 49779
1-800-622-4148

Presque Isle County Historical
  Museum
176 West Michigan Avenue
Rogers City, MI 49779
517-734-4121

Tawas Point State Park
686 Tawas Beach Road
East Tawas, MI 48730
517-362-5041

P. H. Hoeft State Park and
  Thompson's Harbor State Park
US 23 North
Rogers City, MI 49779
517-734-2543

Cheboygan State Park
4490 Beach Road
Cheboygan, MI 49721
616-627-2811

Drive 4

Hartwick Pines State Park
Route 3, POB 3840
Grayling, MI 49738
517-348-7068

Drive 5

Straits State Park
720 Church Street
St. Ignace, MI 49781
906-643-8620

Father Marquette National Memorial
720 Church Street
St. Ignace, MI 49781
906-643-9394

Cheboygan State Park
4490 Beach Road
Cheboygan, MI 49721
616-627-2811

Mackinac State Historic Parks
POB 370
Mackinac Island, MI 49757
616-436-5563

Greater Mackinaw City Chamber of
  Commerce
POB 856
Mackinaw City, MI 49701
616-436-5574

Drive 6

Brimley State Park
Route 2, Box 202
Brimley, MI 49715
906-248-3422

Sault Convention and Visitor's
  Bureau
2581 I-75 Business Spur
Sault Ste. Marie, MI 49783
906-632-3301

Le Sault de Sainte Marie Historical
  Sites
501 East Water Street
Sault Ste. Marie, MI 49783
906-632-3685

Sault Ste. Marie Welcome Center
1001 Eureka Street
Sault Ste. Marie, MI 49783
906-632-8242

Great Lakes Shipwreck Museum
110 Whitefish Point Road
Paradise, MI 49768
906-635-1742

Hiawatha National Forest
USDA Forest Service
4000 I-75 Business Spur
Sault Ste. Marie, MI 49783
906-635-5311

Paradise Area Chamber of Commerce
POB 82
Paradise, MI 49768
906-492-3219

Drive 7

Tahquamenon Falls State Park
Star Route 48
Box 225
Paradise, MI 49768
906-492-3415

Tahquamenon Logging Museum
POB 254
Newberry MI 49868

Newberry Historical Restoration
  Association
POB 254
Newberry MI 49868
906-293-3700

Paradise Area Tourism Council
POB 64
Paradise, MI 49768
906-492-3927

Drive 8

Pictured Rocks National Lakeshore
POB 40 Sand Point Road
Munising, MI 49862
906-387-2607

United States Forest Service
400 East Munising Avenue
Munising, MI 49862
906-387-3700

Drive 9

Seney National Wildlife Refuge
HCR #2, Box 1
Seney, MI 49883
906-586-9851

Drive 10

Van Riper State Park
POB 66
Champion, MI 49814
906-339-4461

Baraga State Park
1300 US 41 South
Baraga, MI 49908
906-353-6558

Marquette County Convention and
  Visitor's Bureau
2552 Highway 41 West, #300
Marquette, MI 49855
906-228-7749

Drive 11

Fort Wilkins State Historic Park
Copper Harbor, MI 49918
906-289-4215

Keweenaw Tourism Council
326 Shelden Avenue
POB 336
Houghton, MI 49931
906-482-2388

Drive 12

Keweenaw Tourism Council
326 Shelden Avenue
POB 336
Houghton, MI 49931
906-482-2388

Drive 13

Ottawa National Forest
Black River Harbor Campground
District Ranger
500 North Moore Street
Bessemer, MI 49911
906-667-0261

Drive 14

Porcupine Mountain Wilderness
  State Park
412 South Boundary Road
Ontonagon, MI 49953
906-885-5275

Ontonagon County Chamber of
  Commerce
POB 266
Ontonagon, MI 49953
906-884-4735

Drive 15

Baraga State Park
1300 US 41 South
Baraga, MI 49908
906-353-6558

Baraga County Tourism and
  Recreation Association
755 East Broad Street
L'Anse, MI 49946

Drive 16

Lake Gogebic State Park
HC 1, POB 139
Marenisco, MI 49947
906-842-3341

Bewabic State Park
1933 US 2 West
Crystal Falls, MI 49920
906-875-3324

Drive 17

Schoolcraft County Chamber of
  Commerce
POB 72
Manistique, MI 49854
906-341-5010

Manisique Area Tourist Council
POB 37
Manistique, MI 49854
906-341-5838

Drive 18

Wilderness State Park
POB 380
Carp Lake, MI 49718
616-436-5381

Mackinaw Area Tourist Bureau
708 South Huron
POB 160
Mackinaw City, MI 49701
616-436-5664

Drive 20

Charlevoix Chamber of Commerce
408 Bridge Street
Charlevoix, MI 49720
616-547-2101

Petoskey State Park
2475 M 119
Petoskey, MI 49712
616-347-2311

Boyne County Convention and
    Visitor's Bureau
401 East Mitchell Street
Petoskey, MI 49770
616-348-2755

Drive 21

Traverse City Area Chamber of
    Commerce
POB 387
Traverse City, MI 49685
616-947-5075

Charlevoix Chamber of Commerce
408 Bridge Street
Charlevoix, MI 49720
616-547-2101

Traverse City State Park
1132 US 31 North
Traverse City, MI 49686
616-922-5270

Fisherman's Island State Park
POB 456, Bells Bay Road
Charlevoix, MI 49720
616-547-6641

Drive 23

Sleeping Bear Dunes National
    Lakeshore
9922 Front Street
Highway M 72
Empire, MI 49630
616-326-5134

Drive 24

Sleeping Bear Dunes National
    Lakeshore
9922 Front Street
Highway M 72
Empire, MI 49630
616-326-5134

Drive 25

Ludington State Park
POB 709, M 116
Ludington, MI 49431
616-843-8671

Manistee Area Chamber of
    Commerce
11 Cypress Street
Manistee, MI 49660
616-723-2575

Manistee Ranger Station
412 Red Apple Road
Manistee, MI 49660
616-723-2211

Ludington Area Chamber of
   Commerce
5827 West US 10
Ludington, MI 49431
616-845-0324

Benzie County Chamber of
   Commerce and Welcome Center
Box 204
Benzonia, MI 49616
616-882-5801

Frankfort Chamber of Commerce
   and Economic Development Office
413 Main Street
Frankfort, MI 49635
616-352-7251

Orchard Beach State Park
2064 Lakeshore Road
Manistee, MI 49660
616-723-7422

Index

About the Author and Photographer

Ed and Kathy-jo Wargin.

Ed and Kathy-jo Wargin specialize in projects that blend their experience and talents as writer and photographer. With a passion for photographing and writing about nature, the couple has created a unique marriage of word and vision.

Both have been active in their careers for more than a decade, serving corporate and commercial clients as well as the publishing and travel industry.

They live in St. Paul, Minnesota, with their son Jake.

get
FALCONGUIDED

A FALCON GUIDE are available for where-to-go hiking, mountain biking, rock climbing, walking, scenic driving, fishing, rockhounding, paddling, birding, wildlife viewing, and camping. We also have FalconGuides on essential outdoor skills and subjects and field identification. The following titles are currently available, but this list grows every year. For a free catalog with a complete list of titles, call FALCON toll-free at 1-800-582-2665.

SCENIC DRIVING GUIDES

Scenic Driving Alaska and the Yukon
Scenic Driving Arizona
Scenic Driving the Beartooth Highway
Scenic Driving California
Scenic Driving Colorado
Scenic Driving Florida
Scenic Driving Georgia
Scenic Driving Hawaii
Scenic Driving Idaho
Scenic Driving Michigan
Scenic Driving Minnesota
Scenic Driving Montana
Scenic Driving New England
Scenic Driving New Mexico
Scenic Driving North Carolina
Scenic Driving Oregon
Scenic Driving the Ozarks including the
   Ouchita Mountains
Scenic Driving Texas
Scenic Driving Utah
Scenic Driving Washington
Scenic Driving Wisconsin
Scenic Driving Wyoming
Back Country Byways
National Forest Scenic Byways
National Forest Scenic Byways II

HISTORIC TRAIL GUIDES

Traveling California's Gold Rush Country
Traveler's Guide to the Lewis & Clark Trail
Traveling the Oregon Trail
Traveler's Guide to the Pony Express Trail

WILDLIFE VIEWING GUIDES

Alaska Wildlife Viewing Guide
Arizona Wildlife Viewing Guide
California Wildlife Viewing Guide
Colorado Wildlife Viewing Guide
Florida Wildlife Viewing Guide
Idaho Wildlife Viewing Guide
Indiana Wildlife Vewing Guide
Iowa Wildlife Viewing Guide
Kentucky Wildlife Viewing Guide
Massachusetts Wildlife Viewing Guide
Montana Wildlife Viewing Guide
Nebraska Wildlife Viewing Guide
Nevada Wildlife Viewing Guide
New Hampshire Wildlife Viewing Guide
New Jersey Wildlife Viewing Guide
New Mexico Wildlife Viewing Guide
New York Wildlife Viewing Guide
North Carolina Wildlife Viewing Guide
North Dakota Wildlife Viewing Guide
Ohio Wildlife Viewing Guide
Oregon Wildlife Viewing Guide
Tennessee Wildlife Viewing Guide
Texas Wildlife Viewing Guide
Utah Wildlife Viewing Guide
Vermont Wildlife Viewing Guide
Virginia Wildlife Viewing Guide
Washington Wildlife Viewing Guide
West Virginia Wildlife Viewing Guide
Wisconsin Wildlife Viewing Guide

FALCON®

■ *To order any of these books, check with your local bookseller or call FALCON® at **1-800-582-2665**.*

Visit us on the world wide web at:
www.falconguide.com

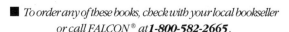

FALCON®

■ *To order any of these books, check with your local bookseller or call FALCON® at **1-800-582-2665**.*

Visit us on the world wide web at:
www.falconguide.com

get
FALCON GUIDED

BIRDING GUIDES
Birding Arizona
Birding Minnesota
Birder's Guide to Montana
Birding Texas
Birding Utah

FIELD GUIDES
Bitterroot: Montana State Flower
Canyon Country Wildflowers
Great Lakes Berry Book
New England Berry Book
Plants of Arizona
Rare Plants of Colorado
Rocky Mountain Berry Book
Southern Rocky Mtn. Wildflowers
Tallgrass Prairie Wildflowers
Western Tree
Wildflowers of Southwestern Utah
Willow Bark and Rosehips

FISHING GUIDES
Fishing Alaska
Fishing the Beartooths
Fishing Florida
Fishing Maine
Fishing Michigan
Fishing Montana

PADDLING GUIDES
Floater's Guide to Colorado
Paddling Montana
Paddling Oregon

HOW-TO GUIDES
Bear Aware
Leave No Trace
Mountain Lion Alert
Wilderness First Aid
Wilderness Survival

ROCK CLIMBING GUIDES
Rock Climbing Colorado
Rock Climbing Montana
Rock Climbing New Mexico
  & Texas
Rock Climbing Utah

ROCKHOUNDING GUIDES
Rockhounding Arizona
Rockhound's Guide to California
Rockhound's Guide to Colorado
Rockhounding Montana
Rockhounding Nevada
Rockhound's Guide to New Mexico
Rockhounding Texas
Rockhounding Utah
Rockhounding Wyoming

WALKING
Walking Colorado Springs
Walking Portland
Walking St. Louis

MORE GUIDEBOOKS
Backcountry Horseman's
  Guide to Washington
Camping California's
  National Forests
Exploring Canyonlands &
  Arches National Parks
Exploring Mount Helena
Recreation Guide to WA
  National Forests
Touring California & Nevada
  Hot Springs
Trail Riding Western
  Montana
Wild Country Companion
Wild Montana
Wild Utah

■ *To order any of these books, check with your local bookseller*
*or call FALCON® at **1-800-582-2665**.*

Visit us on the world wide web at:
www.falconguide.com

FALCON®

MOUNTAIN BIKING GUIDES

Mountain Biking Arizona
Mountain Biking Colorado
Mountain Biking New Mexico
Mountain Biking New York
Mountain Biking Northern New England
Mountain Biking Southern New England
Mountain Biking Utah

Local Cycling Series

Fat Trax Bozeman
Fat Trax Colorado Springs
Mountain Biking Bend
Mountain Biking Boise
Mountain Biking Chequamegon
Mountain Biking Denver/Boulder
Mountain Biking Durango
Mountain Biking Helena
Mountain Biking Moab

FALCON®

■ *To order any of these books, check with your local bookseller
or call FALCON® at **1-800-582-2665**.*

Visit us on the world wide web at:
www.falconguide.com